In the words of the late John F. Ken "The work of TVA will never be over. There will always be new frontiers for it to conquer. For in the minds of men the world over, the initials TVA stand for progress."

President Kennedy made that statement on TVA's thirtieth birthday, May, 1963. Here, looking back on those first thirty years and trying to estimate what may lie ahead, eight specialists set down their thoughts on TVA's impact—its nature, extent, and direction. The essays range from a discussion of the political factors in regional resource development and a review of the controversy surrounding TVA to a broad inquiry into TVA's future.

More specifically, case studies of the Cauca Valley Corporation in Colombia and the Khuzistan Water and Power Authority in Iran demonstrate how TVA serves as a model for other development projects.

Of wide interest is the story, presented here, of the part TVA played in exposing the price-fixing conspiracy in the electrical equipment industry—a scandal that resulted in twenty federal grand jury indictments returned on twenty-nine companies and forty-five executives.

Here also is an examination of TVA's actual impact as compared to its potential impact, its disappointments as well as its achievements. A sound assessment of the problems still confronting TVA bears out the President's remark: "There will always be new frontiers for it to conquer."

This volume grew out of the Fifth University of Tennessee Symposium, held to recog- present work. As a summary of the varying degrees of influence of this prototype for regional resource development, the collection will interest the specialist and the general reader alike.

THE EDITOR

John R. Moore received his Ph.D. in economics at Cornell University and is Professor of Economics at the University of Tennessee. He is Director of the Tennessee Interindustry Study and co-author of *Economics: Principles, Problems and Perspectives.*

The Economic Impact of TVA

THE ECONOMIC IMPACT OF TVA

Edited by JOHN R. MOORE

THE UNIVERSITY OF TENNESSEE PRESS / *Knoxville*

The University of Tennessee and the Department of Economics gratefully acknowledge the financial assistance given by the Sperry and Hutchinson Company Lecture Program in supporting the symposium on which this book is based.

Preface

The University of Tennessee and the Tennessee Valley Authority have engaged in cooperative programs of educational significance for a period spanning more than three decades. A master contract between the two agencies, which was originally limited to agricultural activities, was broadened in 1952 to permit cooperation between TVA and all departments of the University. In addition to formalized projects that under this contract are governed by written agreement, the two institutions have shared staff and facilities over the years in informal undertakings of broad and diverse scope. In 1963, a UT-TVA joint committee was established to coordinate the search for newer ideas for and approaches to mutually rewarding endeavor.

In the spring of 1964, the University's Department of Economics sponsored a symposium in special recognition of the Authority's thirtieth anniversary. The present publication is based principally on the series of public lectures presented on this occasion. A brief review of their scope and content is provided in the "Editor's Introduction." Although this is only one of the many treatises on the Authority, it may be hoped that, for many readers, this book will shed new light on the significance of one of the world's most interesting experiments of government. In addition, the book is intended to reflect the importance that the University of Tennessee attaches to the cooperation and good will which the University and the Authority have shared from the time TVA came into existence.

Robert S. Avery
Assistant Vice President for Academic Affairs
The University of Tennessee

Contents

Editor's Introduction ix

1 Electric Power and Economic Development *by Bruce C. Netschert* 1

2 The Application of TVA Experience to Underdeveloped Countries *by John Oliver* 25

3 Natural Resource Problems and TVA *by Joseph L. Fisher* 41

4 The Politics of Water Resource Development as Exemplified by TVA *by Norman Wengert* 57

5 Identical Pricing and TVA: Toward More Effective Competition *by Ronald H. Wolf* 81

6 An Unfinished Task: A Socio-Economic Evaluation of the TVA Experiment *by Stefan H. Robock* 105

7 Toward More Realistic Assumptions in Regional Economic Development *by Gilbert Banner* 121

8 The Future of TVA *by Aubrey J. Wagner* 145

Index 161

Editor's Introduction

TVA has completed the first thirty years of its existence. It was born in the Muscle Shoals controversy in the twenties and early thirties, and the limelight of controversy has focused with intermittent brilliance upon it during its entire existence. During the fifties it was Dixon-Yates; during the sixties the controversy has been, among other things, responsibility for the plunder of strip mining and the wisdom of constructing the Tellico Dam on the lower reaches of the Little Tennessee River. The controversy has concerned not only TVA itself and its programs but has extended to the evaluation of its direct impact and its importance as a case study of integrated resource development. For example, writing about TVA in 1958, Professor Norton Ginsburg of the University of Chicago observed, "The Tennessee Valley has become the great prototype of river basin development." But he also went on to remark, "It is far from clear whether the TVA provides a suitable model for emulation in much of the less developed world."[1]

In view of this history of disagreement and controversy, it is appropriate, then, that we stand back for a comprehensive look at the economic impact TVA has exerted in the past, is exerting now, and may exert in the future. In making such an evaluation in these days of intense concern with regional economic development, it is only fitting that we ask our questions in the broad framework of the meaning of TVA for the nation as a whole—an inquiry directly relevant to the countries of the world faced with similar regional development problems.

On the occasion of TVA's twentieth anniversary, another summary volume was published jointly by the University of Alabama Press and the University of Tennessee Press. The present publication differs substantially from the previous one. The earlier book was written by then members of the TVA staff; and it attempted to cover, in broad fashion, the many facets of TVA operations. The present volume, consisting of eight papers, is the outcome of the Fifth University of Tennessee Symposium, held in recognition of TVA's thirtieth anniversary. The theme of this symposium was "The Economic Impact of TVA," and the six participants invited to present lectures at that time were selected on the basis of their ability to contribute to an evaluation of TVA. In fact, the group of experts consisted of one present employee (the chairman of the Board of Directors) and three who formerly were associated with the organization. In addition to the two papers by those never associated with the TVA are two papers, not presented at the symposium, which were prepared by members of the University of Tennessee Department of Economics.

This volume begins with a consideration of the general question of the role of electrical energy in economic development and moves on to a discussion and evaluation of the role that TVA has played in a number of important areas: in transferring know-how to underdeveloped areas, in developing natural resources, in illustrating the politics of water resource development, and in the area (perhaps surprisingly) of antitrust. There follow two papers which attempt to assess in broad terms where TVA has been and to indicate possible lines of further development. The final essay is an inquiry into TVA's future by its board chairman. Those who find fault with this organization will find it easy to substitute their own judgment for that of the editor, since each of these essays stands by itself and the individual contributions can be read in any order without doing violence to the coherence of the discussion.

A brief introduction to the individual papers may be of interest to those who wish to read these papers selectively. Bruce Netschert's contribution concerns the role played by energy sources generally and electric power in particular in programs of economic development. The argument is advanced and documented that large-scale power development is not a panacea. It was not so in the case of TVA, and it is perhaps less likely to be for other areas. The author concludes that a preoccupation with the development of thermal and hydro generating stations in the early stages of economic development is an unwise allocation of capital. This essay is "must" reading for the planning authorities in underdeveloped areas.

The paper by John Oliver, former general manager of TVA and now president of Development and Resources Corporation, continues in the vein of evaluating the applicability of TVA experience to the underdeveloped areas. Oliver argues that the uniqueness of TVA—the aspect of TVA which excites and interests its many visitors—is "the basic concept and philosophy of the program," not the details of its operating procedures or its approaches to the solution of specific or isolated problems. After pointing out the important philosophical and organizational attributes which a TVA counterpart in an underdeveloped area must have and the difficulties which might be encountered in establishing these prerequisites, Mr. Oliver gives us two case studies showing problems and procedures involved in establishing two development agencies modeled, essentially, after TVA: the Cauca Valley Corporation in Colombia and the Khuzistan Water and Power Authority in Iran.

Joseph Fisher places his discussion of TVA in the context of the changing problems of natural resource availability and utilization which face the United States as a whole. The discussion points up the contribution that TVA has made toward a solution to some of these resource problems. Fisher discusses the nature of many of the problems which remain. In general, he feels that a regional approach to the solution of these problems can make major contributions. While feeling that perhaps some experimentation with organizational structures might be desirable, he suggests that it would also be interesting to see the development of more regional agencies patterned after the broad multipurpose format of TVA.

In the fourth essay, Professor Norman Wengert, examining the development of TVA, notes that water resource development was and is largely pragmatic rather than ideological. In this connection, Wengert makes a number of interesting comments on the controversy which has raged with varying degrees of intensity on the issue of TVA and socialism. He notes that TVA has been singled out from a number of other government programs for attack and suggests that perhaps this is the price TVA has had to pay for its very success in meeting its objectives. As Wengert states, "TVA shows that government need not be inefficient and bumbling. . . ." He argues that this and other controversies have proven to be a good thing; controversy exposes the issues to public view and permits the decision-making process to be carried on in public, as is proper in a democratic society.

The next contribution also illustrates an important but often overlooked contribution which TVA has made to the nation. This paper by Ronald Wolf, which is supplementary to those presented at the symposium, looks at the recent role of TVA in promoting competition in the private sector of the economy. Professor Wolf offers a detailed examination of activities of TVA in exposing the bid-rigging which involved many major producers of electrical equipment who were supposedly selling to the agency on a competitive-bid basis. This is the story of the fascinating details of what is certain to go down in antitrust history as a landmark case.

The contributions by Stefan H. Robock and by Gilbert Banner are concerned specifically with the problem of evaluating TVA. Dr. Robock argues that no really systematic evaluation of the social and economic impact of TVA is presently available. In effect, his essay is a prospectus for such an evaluation. In setting forth how such a comprehensive evaluation might be undertaken, he gives us important, usually unrecognized insights into the nature of TVA's impact.

Professor Banner's essay was not presented at the symposium but is presented here to round out the original contributions. His stance is essentially that of the friendly critic of TVA. Obviously sympathetic to TVA in its over-all conception, he raises a number of questions concerning the direction, scope, and force of TVA's activities. In many areas he finds shortcomings in the TVA record.

He points out that, in part, these may be explained by the failure of TVA itself. But, more important may be the shortcomings of the legislative process in defining the scope of TVA activities and the changing nature of the national economic system—the context in which TVA operates. Many of the developments of the last twenty years have created an environment with which an agency of the nature of TVA cannot be expected to cope; if regional resource development is to be pursued, substantial changes may be necessary in the institutional arrangements through which we approach such problems.

Appropriately enough, the final contribution on the future of the TVA is the work of Board Chairman Aubrey J. Wagner. Chairman Wagner examines the potential contribution which TVA can make for the benefit of the people of the Valley region and of the nation as a whole. These benefits embrace a number of specific areas: electric power, orderly development of lake-shore lands, flood control, the development of industrial and recreational sites, forestry, and agriculture. This listing, of course, coincides generally with the objectives laid out for TVA thirty years ago, thus indicating that there is probably no area of its earlier activity to which "finished" can be written. The major difference between the situation then and now is that there are more highly developed institutions now available for dealing with these problems. TVA has, justifiably, become known the world around as *the* institution standing for and promoting progress in regional resource development.

Are there any generalizations which emerge when these eight papers are considered as a whole? Although drawing broad conclusions from so diverse a group of essays by such a heterogeneous group of contributors may be dangerous, it may also be worthwhile for just these reasons. It is, of course, easy to conclude that all these authors admire the achievements of TVA during its first thirty years. Though some would have had TVA seize the initiative more boldly, most, I believe, would conclude that TVA's successes have been greater than might have been hoped for a generation ago. On the other hand, these men do not seem to believe that TVA's success has been great enough to recommend its form of administrative organization for regional resource development as the only basis for approaching the problems of tomorrow in the United States and abroad. Why not? There seem to be a number of factors indicated, some explicitly, some implicitly.

First, the heart of the TVA operation is electric power generation; when this means the displacement of private power operations, as is necessarily the case in the United States, it also means that the entire organization and all of its activities come under attack. Such an attack is bound to have its effect either through adverse legislation and litigation—and resultant diversion of the organization's energy to meeting the attack—or through a creeping exhaustion on the part of those who have fought a good fight for years but who, perhaps unknowingly, gradually tend to avoid further controversy by modifying their original objectives.

Second, there seems to be the feeling that the scope of TVA's authority as defined by Congress may be too restricted to make possible anything more than the simple development of natural resources; in other words, integrated development which is more broadly based has not been possible. The TVA emphasis made perfectly logical economic sense in a world that accepted the classical dictum of Say's Law that "supply creates its own demand." According to this approach, resource development is economic progress. But in the economic world transformed by Keynesian emphasis on effective demand, the TVA format for development may be seriously inadequate. Thus, whereas the TVA approach may still be an appropriate way to secure development in a nation of underdeveloped stature, it is likely to be outmoded in a developed nation which, to use Rostow's phrases, has reached the stage of "high mass consumption" or "maturity." While the elimination of the pockets of poverty in such a developed economy may involve the expansion of the resource base, it must, in most cases, require considerably more than that. Thus, pursuit of the goal of integrated regional development, so well advanced by TVA under its limited objectives, requires the development of new agencies and institutions with a broader focus than that conceived by the founders of TVA a generation ago.

JOHN R. MOORE
Professor of Economics
The University of Tennessee

References

1. Norton S. Ginsburg, "The Regional Concept and Planning Regions," in United Nations, *Regional Planning: Seminar on Regional Planning, Tokyo, 28 July to 8 August 1958* (New York: United Nations, 1959), pp. 39, 40.

Electric Power and Economic Development

BRUCE C. NETSCHERT holds B.A. and Ph.D. degrees from Cornell University. After a brief stint of teaching at the University of Minnesota, Dr. Netschert served from 1951 to 1955 in government posts. From 1955 to 1961 he was a resource economist with Resources for the Future. Since 1961 he has been Director of the Washington Office of National Economic Research Associates. Among Dr. Netschert's publications are: *Future Supply of Oil and Gas*, *General Geology for Colleges* (co-author), and *Energy in the American Economy.*

A discussion of electric power and economic development may best begin with a brief look at the role that energy plays in economic development. At the outset, a distinction should be made between the terms "economic development" and "economic growth." Development, not unnaturally, takes place in circumstances of underdevelopment, as in what it is now fashionable to call the "underdeveloped countries." Underdevelopment may also exist within advanced economies in regions of lagging growth that exhibit such symptoms as chronic unemployment, an income level severely lower than the average for the economy as a whole, and underdeveloped (or depleted) resources.

Economic development may be described as a process of increasing economic activity, in which total income and, hopefully, per capita income as well are expanded—all of these things being at low levels, both in absolute terms and in relation to the levels of advanced, industrialized countries. Economic growth is, of course, involved in the process; but the crux of the problem in underdeveloped countries and regions is the breaking out from a growth rate that has always been low, and achieving instead a very high growth rate.

In contrast, the advanced economy exists by reason of previous satisfactory growth. The problem in this instance is not (at least for the economy as a whole) one of raising a low per capita income but of raising or at least maintaining an already high one. Growth alone, in other words, in the sense of an expansion of total income, is sufficient as a minimum. In the underdeveloped situation, growth alone in this sense is not enough. Therefore we shall associate the term "development" with the underdeveloped situation and the term "growth" with the advanced economy.

In the period since World War II a great deal of attention has been given throughout the world to the role of energy in economic development. This attention has stemmed, in turn, from the high level of interest in the subject of economic development itself. Much of this interest has been generated by the ever-growing disparity between the material well-being of the inhabitants of underdeveloped and of advanced countries. It has been fostered by the international activities of the United Nations and its allied organizations, notably in the many meetings and conferences that have been held under its auspices. Since the proceedings of the 1955 Geneva Conference on the Peaceful Uses of Atomic Energy first captured the imagination of the world, there has been a series of international gatherings which have considered not only the subject of economic development but the relation of energy supply and use to economic development. At the same time, interest in the subject of economic growth has also been high in the advanced countries, where the maintenance of a satisfactorily high growth rate has emerged as a prime social goal and where the means and techniques of achieving that goal have become political issues. In addition, the advanced countries have also turned their attention to the problems of their internal regions of underdevelopment.

One of the few points of agreement in all that has been written on the role of energy in economic development and growth appears to be the proposition that there is a strong correlation between the level of income and the level of energy use in a region or country. A standard item in discussion of the subject has been the scatter diagram demonstrating the correlation between per capita energy consumption and per capita national income throughout the world. It has also been recognized that the mere availability of energy in abundance does not in itself assure a high per capita income level, as the circumstances of the petroleum-rich countries of the Persian Gulf and the hydro-rich countries of Africa demonstrate. Indeed, it has been observed that most high-income countries consume more fuels than they produce and most low-income countries produce more fuels than they consume.[1]

Nevertheless, the exact relation of energy use to economic development and growth remains a matter of dispute. There seems to be no question that growth is accompanied by increased energy use; the highest rate of growth in U. S. energy consumption, for example, was in the period 1850–1910, when this country was building its industrial base.[2] Investigators of the relationship in many countries have used regression analysis to obtain coefficients which show that for each additional unit of national income X units of energy were consumed, but there has been no agreement on what these results mean. "Depending on what has to be proved, energy consumption has variously been expounded as a function of the national product, or—in a liberal interpretation—of the living standard or, on the contrary, the level of the national product as a result of a more or less elevated energy consumption."[3]

There has also been no clear-cut relation discernible between the cost of energy and the role of energy in economic development and growth. To some, the high cost of energy in many underdeveloped regions and countries is one of the chief obstacles, if not the greatest one, to economic development. Some believe, however, that other economic or social circumstances are responsible for the underdevelopment.

My own view of the role of energy in economic development and growth is well expressed in the following quotation:

> Although [the] share of energy costs amounts approximately to less than 10% of the value of gross national production and to about 5% of the value of industrial production, the price of energy nevertheless represents [an] important factor in economic development. . . . The obstacles which lead to expensive production of energy can be, however, compensated by [the] favourable situation of other factors of production. There is therefore no clear correlation between the prices of energy and national revenue in spite of high correlation between energy consumption and national income. This proves the earlier conclusion that the level of energy production cannot be considered as a direct cause of the amount of national income, but it is more likely that production of energy and the amount of national income have common cause in the size of capital formation.[4]

Electric Power in Economic Development and Growth

If the role of energy in economic development and growth is indeterminate, what of the role of electric power? Here, too, there is the same general correlation between level of income and level of power consumption; but since electricity is only one of several forms of energy input it is obvious that wide variation will exist between economies and regions, depending on the proportion of total energy input that is in the form of electric power.

It is recognized, nevertheless, that to a large extent efficient industry is dependent on electric power; and to the extent that the individual consumer is able to use power directly, his standard of living is higher. Power, then, can contribute to economic development; but to what extent is power a prerequisite to any development, a catalyst which in small quantities can have large results? Or to what extent is power merely one of the many things that seem to go along with economic development?

According to one view *cheap* power *is* a prerequisite. In the words of a Pakistani civil servant, "One of the main obstacles in the development of industries in underdeveloped countries is the shortage of cheap electric power. This is the most dynamic factor for industrial development. The importance of industrialization in underdeveloped countries, particularly where shortage of land seriously impedes agricultural development, needs no emphasis."[5]

The opposite view is expressed by Philip Sporn: "In general the use of electric energy is determined by complex economic and noneconomic factors, only one of which is the cost of electric energy and of the primary fuel for its generation. Much more important factors in determining the establishment and expansion of energy-consuming industries are markets, transportation costs, location of raw materials for processing, and so on. Rarely is it true to say that the cost of electric energy determines the character of an economy."[6]

Obviously, the cost of energy cannot be disregarded. If, for example, as may be true in many underdeveloped countries, the kilowatt-hour cost of electricity is significantly greater than the cost of its labor equivalent, the electric power is not going to contribute much to economic development.[7] Nevertheless, there are, I think, several things wrong with the point of view that cheap power is either a prerequisite to or the vital catalyst in economic development.

Leaving aside for the moment the legitimacy of identifying economic development with industrialization, especially heavy industry, one can point to many examples, such as Niagara Falls and Schaffhausen, Switzerland, where prime hydro sites have attracted a concentration of energy-intensive industry through the availability of bulk power at low cost. One can point to other instances, such as Kitimat in British Columbia, where bulk, low-cost power was developed as part of the siting of an energy-intensive industrial process. But is this economic development as it applies to underdeveloped regions and countries? How has the *general* development of British Columbia benefited from the Kitimat project? How would the future *general* development of Alaska benefit from the Rampart project?

There is, in fact, evidence to the contrary—that low-cost power is not necessarily a magnet for industry nor important in economic development. Such evidence exists in the Tennessee Valley. Let me quote from the 1959 Annual Report of the TVA:

> TVA's resource development activities have contributed to the growth in industry as, for example, in the improvement of water transportation, ample supplies of electricity, and improved use of soil, forest, and mineral resources which provide the basis for expansion. However, this expansion has not taken place at the expense of other areas where industry also has grown, and often with the help of the same kind of resource development activity carried on by the Federal Government through other agencies. New businesses have been formed by individuals and firms in the TVA area and new branch plants of companies operating nationwide have been built. Such new enterprises have been attracted for the usual complex of reasons—nearness to markets, availability of raw materials, plentiful labor supply, transportation and communication facilities, and others.
>
> Loosely made charges that low-cost power has lured industry away or "pirated" companies and plants from other areas have collapsed when facts were faced. In view of the continued complaints, TVA recently conducted a survey to discover the facts about the alleged migration of industry. During the 19 years from 1940 through 1958, the survey indicated, 25 firms ceased operations in areas outside the TVA region and relocated here. They represented employment of 3,800 people. During the same period, 9 firms representing an employment of 2,000 persons left the TVA region for locations elsewhere. The net gain of 16 plants and 1,800 employees was negligible in the total growth of industry in the region. . . .[8]

The TVA was here concerned with rebutting charges of industrial piracy, but it is clear that the role of power in the development of the Tennessee Valley region was not dominant. Power was not the catalyst but merely one of many things in the TVA program that contributed to the regional development and made that development the stunning success it has been.

The argument that power must be cheap if it is to be used at all in underdeveloped countries implies that where local power is *not* available, it is because power could be made available only at high cost. This implication flies in the face of the numerous instances where power *is* available at high cost, as in the capital and perhaps other large cities of many of the most abysmally underdeveloped countries. With power, even expensive power, *some* economic activities are possible that would otherwise be impossible.

Admittedly, the demand for power is most unlikely to be inelastic with respect to price; more power would be consumed if it were available at a lower price, and such additional power consumption would presumably result in much more economic activity or real income. But I would make a distinction between the desirability of choosing among available alternatives so as to provide power—like any important economic input—at the lowest possible total outlay, and the necessity of cheap power for economic development, which may involve very large total outlay. The latter choice may well be an inefficient use of capital.

Before leaving the subject of the general role of power in economic development and growth, it is instructive to look at the circumstances of the introduction of power into the advanced economies of the Western world. At first glance this would seem to have little relevance to the present and future. The United States and the industrialized nations of western Europe were already intensive energy consumers, with an industrialization based largely on steam power. That is, their industries used machinery run by mechanical linkage with steam engines.

There is at present no nation at any stage of industrialization whose energy is steam powered, and it is inconceivable that any nation in the future will industrialize, to even the slightest degree, on a steam-power basis. The introduction of electric power under these same circumstances is thus a thing of the past, but at least two aspects of that historical experience are worth noting. The first is that it was autogenous: it happened of itself; it was not initiated, fostered, or stimulated as a political or social policy. As I see it, such autogenous occurrence is significant in that electric power, once introduced, expanded more or less apace with demand growth. There was not, as there is in many economies today, a public aware of but unable to secure the benefits of electric power. Nor was there, as in other economies today, an initial availability of power from enormous blocks of generating capacity in excess of existing demand.

In other words, electric power, when introduced under such circumstances, started small—very small—and grew gradually but steadily, by small accretions. The current needs for mechanical power, as I have pointed out, were already being met. Thus it was inevitable that the growth would be in small increments relative to total power consumption. The technical journals of that era make fascinating reading. On the one hand, power plants were being installed in individual factories and establishments. On the other, central stations were being built by adventurous entrepreneurs who scoured the surrounding country for customers to tie to their lines, gradually convincing even the factory owners of the economic and other advantages of central-station generation.

Thus the process of electrification took care of itself, largely because electricity was able to supplant an already satisfactory (but not *as* satisfactory) power supply. The point is, however, that *the installation of power capacity took place in small increments.*

Initially, the electrification of industry consisted merely of replacing a prime mover with an electric motor and retaining the jungle of transmission belts and pulleys to transmit power to individual machines. Gradually, however, in a process that extended in this country into the 1920's, electric motors were incorporated into separate machines. According to the findings of the Resources for the Future study of energy in the American economy:

> the growing use of electric motors in manufacturing and the improvements in electrical control equipment brought with them a flexibility in industrial operations previously impossible to achieve. Before the advent of the electric motor, mechanical power, where needed, had to be obtained for the single prime mover in the plant no matter how small the needs might be. Manufacturing operations thus had to be designed to accommodate the location of the machines to that of the prime mover . . . rather than to the sequence of the production process. The introduction of the unit drive, in which each machine has its own motor or motors, changed all this: power was available in completely flexible form, and could be distributed throughout the factory in accord with other criteria of efficient organization. . . .
>
> It seems probable, therefore, that the greatest impact of electricity on the efficiency of industrial operations was achieved . . . in terms of electricity's impact on the total economics of industrial operations. The release from the restrictions of internal mechanical energy transmission systems opened up wholly new possibilities for applying modern techniques of industrial and business management. It is, therefore, not far-fetched to speculate that the marked acceleration in the increase in labor and capital productivity after World War I is attributable in some degree to the new methods of organizing production made possible through the growing electrification of industrial operations.[9]

The Capital Requirements of Power

It is probably not an exaggeration to say that the capital requirements present the greatest difficulties in actually providing power to underdeveloped countries. These countries are capital poor to begin with, and the fact that capital in large quantities is required for almost all aspects of economic development merely intensifies the problem. By contrast, in underdeveloped regions within advanced economies, there is no such problem; and this constitutes one of the most significant distinctions between the two sets of circumstances.

The more spectacular and familiar occurrence of the problem is the need for very large capital investments in the development of individual hydro sites. Here the need is commonly altogether beyond the ability of the economy to meet, whether through private or public means. But even in the case of fossil-fueled central stations of moderate size the capital needs are large, and in the smaller stations in which diesel generation may be applied the capital requirements per unit of output are high. Indeed, because of the economies of scale associated with power production, the smaller the installation the higher the unit capital costs.

Troublesome as this is, it is only the beginning of the problem. As Daniel and Robinson have observed, the capital employed in an industrialized economy "consists largely of engines and machines and . . . these are largely devices for using energy"[10]; moreover, industries which use a great deal of power are also the most capital intensive. Thus the use of capital to provide power for industrialization only augments the capital problem. The investment of capital in power generation is usually just a fraction of the investment in power-consuming industry; hence, investment in power generation for industrialization merely leads to much larger investment needs.[11] The view quoted earlier, that power is the prerequisite for industrialization, therefore misstates the case. Although power may be one of the initial requirements, this need is submerged in the larger over-all requirement for capital.

Here we have the nub of the situation. If supplied to an underdeveloped country, power cannot act automatically as a catalyst in bringing about industrialization as that term is commonly understood. Where industrialization is practicable to begin with, power may facilitate the process; but as a piece of investment power is unlikely to lead to the automatic chain of events that results in growth in the already developed economy.

Moreover, there is a lesson here regarding attempts to apply the TVA experience to underdeveloped countries on the theory that its success in this country demonstrates that it will succeed wherever applied. What the power aspect of TVA contributed to the development and economic growth of the Tennessee Valley region was possible only because of the large additional investment that was made spontaneously within an economy in which there was no scarcity of capital.

We are not speaking here of the other accomplishments of TVA, such as reforestation, inland navigation, and the general improvement of agricultural practices—all of which, very likely, have contributed more to the regional development than power alone. But the popular identification in this country of TVA with power may well have carried over in the application of the TVA approach in other parts of the world.

Certainly this view of power as only a minor aspect of TVA existed at the outset. President Roosevelt's message to Congress on TVA stated, for example, "It is clear that the Muscle Shoals development is but a small part of the potential public usefulness of the entire Tennessee River. Such use, if envisioned in its entirety, transcends mere power development."[12]

The Goal of Power Development and Means of Achievement

There can be little disagreement with the proposition that the ultimate goal of power development is the provision of social benefits to the population of a country or region. These benefits may be accomplished either directly, through the improvement of the individual's standard of living by his use of power, or indirectly, through the general growth in income levels as a result of improved productivity and the growth of economic activity.

Consider first the indirect approach, through improved productivity. Again, the earlier quotation on the results of the electrification of U. S. industry is apt. The passage describes a process which in some measure applies also to existing industry in underdeveloped countries where electric power is lacking. Even greater results accrue, of course, where inanimate power has not previously been used, as in small manufacturing operations done by hand,[13] and in agricultural processing, such as milling, previously employing animal power. (In underdeveloped regions in advanced economies an example would be the use of electric milking machines in dairy farming.)

Still another effect on agricultural productivity, which can be profound, results from the provision of power for irrigation pumping. All in all, however, it is likely that the productivity increase resulting from electrification would be less in agriculture than in industry. Most of the increase in agricultural productivity in this century throughout the world has been due to other things, including mechanization, scientific breeding, fertilizing, and pest control.

Another indirect means of enhancing living standards is the use of previously unused resources. At first glance, one might think there are countless examples of this in the exploitation of isolated mineral deposits, both in the industrialized and underdeveloped countries. To be sure, such exploitation cannot take place without electric power, but I am forced to conclude that in almost every instance it is more nearly a case of the chicken coming before the egg. The decision is made to exploit the deposit and power is made available in order to do so, the power supply being created for that purpose alone. In fact, I cannot point to a single instance in which a previously known mineral deposit lay unexploited until power became available through the installation of capacity for general purposes or other specific purposes. Where mineral deposits *have* been exploited long after their existence was first known, it has been because of factors other than the new availability of power. The exploitation of the bauxite deposits of Australia may, however, turn out to be a valid example.

Still a third means is the attraction of power-intensive industries through the provision of bulk, low-cost power. This situation in advanced economies has previously been referred to; but even where this approach has proved successful, as in the Pacific Northwest, its applicability as a catalyst in the underdeveloped country—and, indeed, in most if not all underdeveloped regions in advanced economies—remains doubtful in my mind. For such a situation to contribute generally to economic development, more than the presence of a single electrometallurgical or electromechanical establishment is necessary. There need be more than one such establishment, and the power-intensive industry should attract to the same region the secondary and tertiary industries that constitute full economic development. Not a single instance of this occurring in an underdeveloped country comes to mind.

Let me give an example. In Cameroon in Equatorial Africa, the French installed a hydro project of 152 mw capacity for a

45,000-ton aluminum plant. In a paper describing this project in 1957, it was claimed that the result would be the local creation of an economic complex involving some 1,000 people based on the income generated by the direct employment of 250 Africans and 70 Europeans in the plant.[14] This is in a country with a population of some four million.

The value of such a project for an underdeveloped country is not denied for a minute. Every little bit counts, including the small surplus power made available for local consumption outside the aluminum works. But the idea that this has a significant effect on income levels and economic development in the total economy (except, perhaps, where the employment is a significant portion of the total labor force) seems to me to be an exaggeration. If outside capital wants to come and do this sort of thing, fine; but more—much more—than this is necessary for the real economic development of Cameroon. This alone will not start the development process. The attraction of power-intensive industries is an inefficient means of general economic development.

There is also the all-too-prevalent idea that power will produce industrialization; this follows from the misconception that economic development is synonymous with industrialization. This misconception is still endemic in the underdeveloped countries, though we may be leaving the era of the prestige steel mill. To be sure, no one among the army of academic, technical, and administrative people engaged in aiding the underdeveloped countries holds the naïve view that a steel mill *ipso facto* constitutes industrialization. Yet the planning and development ministry of many an underdeveloped country cherishes the idea of heavy industry. "A warning has to be sounded against the concentration of a few big and costly plants which consume all the capital and hydro-electric power of the region. Excessive emphasis on industry for industry's sake, above all heavy industry, may leave an underdeveloped country with the symbol of development rather than the substance."[15]

Finally, there is the indirect method of achieving the social goal of electrification by the inauguration of new light industry.

There are three advantages here: First, there is a market, however small, for many consumer goods in all underdeveloped countries. Second, the light industries are not capital intensive; hence, with an available power supply, their local inauguration is less difficult. And third, the light industries are not energy intensive, so that a modest power supply will suffice for their establishment. The significance of these advantages is that they encourage autogenous increase in income generation as a result of electrification. Indeed, it is difficult to visualize the provision of electric power in an underdeveloped country (that is, power not dedicated in advance to specific use in a heavy-industry project) which would not be followed by the blossoming of *some* light industry.

Turning now to the direct approach—or the raising of consumer living standards by the consumer's use of power—it would appear at first glance that here, too, there are special advantages. Except for large cities (which can be disregarded, since in every country such cities have power service of some sort) the small power requirements of the individual consumer mean that even in the aggregate the consumer can be supplied with power at a relatively small investment. In small towns and in villages the capital requirements are extremely modest. Moreover, in these rural areas, which generally lack any electric power whatever, the provision of power can mean an enormous difference in the standard of living. Electric lighting and radios are immediate possibilities.

These advantages may well be more apparent than real, however. Here are the sobering and perspicacious remarks of a spokesman from Malaya:

> rural electricity *solely* for providing additional social amenity is uneconomical in tropical countries, where there is no requirement for space heating and daylight hours are long and constant throughout the year. To poor villagers, an electric supply is considered a luxury and takes second place after more essential requirements like pipe water and good access roads. Rural electrification, unless accompanied by semi-industrial demand, such as irrigation pumping and processing of agricultural products, is a luxury underdeveloped countries, with low investment resources, can ill afford. The debatable question is whether,

under the circumstances, it should be subsidized by other consumers in the country, thus running the risk of retarding the growth of electricity expansion in the rest of the country.[16]

There is nothing with which to take exception in these remarks. They make the point conclusively that whatever direct benefits may be contributed to the consumer standard of living by electrification should be viewed as a byproduct of electrification for other purposes, and not as an end in itself.

Interestingly, this point is also applicable to rural electrification in the advanced economy. Here it is more than a mere matter of lighting and radio and television. It can mean a refrigerator instead of an icebox, a vacuum cleaner instead of a carpet sweeper, an electric churn instead of a hand one, or all the infinite variety of household electrical appliances available. Nevertheless, the effect of electrification on the rural standard of living is really dependent on the level of money income, because it is not the cost of electricity that determines how the consumer will use the available power, but the cost of the appliance.[17] This does not minimize in the slightest the accomplishments of rural electrification in this country and in Europe; but it does suggest, as with TVA, that experience here cannot be extrapolated to the underdeveloped country. The success of rural electrification in the United States was basically due to the fact that it took place in a high-income economy.

The Energy Source

The source of energy for power generation is also an important aspect in the provision of power for economic development. This involves not only the obvious matter of the presence or absence of indigenous energy sources, but also the relation between the energy source and such things as the required investment and the scale of generation as well.

Consider, to begin with, the use of vegetable fuels, such as bagasse and wood, which has frequently been associated with the initial stages of power production in an underdeveloped country.

The supply of bagasse or other agricultural waste is quite inelastic, as it is for any such byproduct, and can thus be used only for small-scale power generation. Wood, on the other hand, may be available in large quantity, but its use for any but small-scale generation is impracticable because of the large gathering and handling operations that would be required.

The use of coal is almost wholly a matter of its indigenous occurrence. It is, of course, lacking in all but a very few of the underdeveloped countries (one might say almost by definition), and its high cost of transport in comparison to oil has ruled it out of consideration as an import. It is safe to say that the presence or absence of indigenous coal or its availability through imports is of little significance in the provision of new power capacity in the underdeveloped countries.

The role of natural gas in power development is curious. In underdeveloped countries where it is associated with abundant crude oil, as in the Middle East, the gas is either used as refinery fuel, returned to the earth to aid in oil recovery, or blown to the atmosphere. The abundance of oil, which is so much more easily handled, leads to the disregard of gas as fuel for central power generation. But in underdeveloped countries where gas is not associated with oil, as in Pakistan, no significant electrification appears to have resulted. Although the emerging technique of liquefied natural gas transport by tanker will undoubtedly result in large-scale international movement of natural gas in the future, the costs will remain so high that gas transported by such means cannot be considered as boiler fuel for central-station power generation.

Fuel oil is now the "universal" fuel, in the sense that its consumption is most widely distributed throughout the world. For those countries with indigenous resources the result may be an ample fuel supply for power generation. One should not generalize too broadly, however. The most suitable petroleum fuel for large central-station use is residual fuel oil, the residual left over from crude oil refining operations. This product has the lowest value of the fuels produced in refining; but it also has the severe disadvantage of high viscosity, which makes it difficult to handle. At moderate and low temperatures residual fuel oil must be heated in order to flow. It thus tends to be available only in locations accessible by water transportation. But since most large cities in the world are either seaports or river ports, it is likely that the major city or cities of any underdeveloped country having a seacoast will have access to residual fuel oil.

Another petroleum product, diesel oil, has special significance for the introduction of electric power into underdeveloped countries. As a refined product, it is higher priced than residual fuel oil but is more easily transported. Its great advantage, though, is its use in diesel engines, which are the best prime movers for very small power plants.

> Experience has shown that, where in developing areas a beginning of public electricity supply is warranted, a sound procedure is to install diesel generators say of 1000 to 1500 Kw unit size. . . . By the time the demand for power has reached say 7/8000 Kw the future development and requirements of the area would be clearer cut and it should be possible to make a full economic study of the relative advantages of separate power stations with individual networks, or possibly a wider network with one major central steam turbine or hydroelectric station. If it should be decided to build such a central station the diesel generators could be picked up and installed in some other area where electricity supply is beginning to be required.[18]

Diesel oil does not, however, offer advantages only. Except where it is available from indigenous resources (which is more the exception than the rule), the use of diesel oil introduces the problem of foreign exchange. For most underdeveloped countries the difficulty of obtaining sufficient foreign exchange for all import needs is chronic. The introduction of diesel-generated power may, therefore, like the provision of power for heavy industry development, create a bigger problem than it solves.

For a brief period it looked as though the answer to this dilemma had appeared in the form of nuclear power. Even though the nuclear fuel would have to be imported in almost every instance, its extremely high energy content, as has been pointed out repeatedly, offers the promise of power with relatively small foreign-exchange requirements. This promise remains, but it has yet to be realized. One explanation for the delay in bringing nuclear power to underdeveloped countries (and a bitter disappointment it has been for many of them) seems to be the difficulty of reducing a wholly new technology to the routine level. As the industrialized countries have found, in the absence of experience it is still necessary to overdesign in order to provide sufficient safety and reliability factors. The result has been much higher investment costs than for the equivalent fossil-fueled station.

A second explanation lies in the high cost of nuclear power on a small scale. It will be a long time (if ever) before small-scale nuclear power costs will approach those of fossil-fueled power, even in areas where the latter costs are high. The advantage of nuclear power is the economy that can be realized at very large scale, but the first cautious extensions into the large-size range are only now being made in the advanced countries.

In addition, the stage has not yet been reached at which a nuclear plant can be installed in an underdeveloped country by the manufacturer's engineers (who are, of course, from an industrialized country) and then turned over to local engineers for use after the usual break-in period. It would be as if Edison, in the first few years of his experience in operating a central power station, had considered installing plants in Latin America, Africa, and Asia—or, for that matter, eastern Europe.

This brings us to hydropower, the remaining energy source. "It seems to be inherent in the thinking of many local governments that power from falling water, no matter what the first investment, is the way to industrial development."[19] Hydropower is not, of course, a panacea for the social and economic problems of any region or country. And it is unfortunately true that hydro development is, as the economist terms it, "lumpy"; in general, it has to be done in a big way if it is to be done at all. Indeed, many of the opportunities for hydro development are so large that even in countries with a tradition of private investment in power facilities only the government has sufficient financial resources to undertake them. In underdeveloped countries, where investment funds from any source are all too scarce, opportunities for hydro development are often beyond even the capacity of the local government to finance and it has become the practice to obtain the financing from other governments or international lending authorities. Even if domestic or foreign private lending institutions were willing to finance the large hydro possibilities, however, it would be at prohibitive terms. Meeting the stringent amortization requirements and high interest rates of private institutions would be difficult enough in local currency; in foreign currencies the balance-of-payments problems with private borrowing would almost certainly be insuperable. Thus it is that the international loans made for hydro development in the postwar era of international cooperation carry generous debt service provisions, such as long moratoria on amortization and perhaps interest, and low interest rates.

But this, of course, is not the whole story. The other side of the hydro coin is the multipurpose project. When flood control, irrigation water, navigability, and other benefits accrue from a hydro project, the tremendous investment in the dam and other structures need not be charged wholly to the power produced. This advantage is offset to a varying degree, however, by the conflicting interests between use of the water for power and for other purposes. Depending on the circumstances of the project, the usability of hydropower may be seriously impaired by such needs as irrigation and flood control.

Like any natural resource, hydro potential frequently suffers the disadvantage of not being where it ought to be and of not occurring on the right scale. Thus, it is quite likely that the provision of power through a large hydro project would necessitate either getting the power to the population centers, where it could best be used, or bringing industry to the power source so that it might be used. The former solution, it should be noted, is really possible only in a country with an already developed power network, and even then the problem is not easily solved. Only through the push into extra high voltage has Sweden been able to make maximum use of its hydro resources and has Canada been able to develop its remote resources.

This is of special significance for underdeveloped countries. It may have been determined that industrialization is desirable for the development of a country; but it is also likely that the hydropower which may be made available will not be so situated that it can effectively contribute to that industrialization. The "solution," in many instances, has been to bring in a highly power-intensive industry, such as aluminum refining; but as already emphasized, this is not a very effective means of stimulating economic development.

The Scale and Pace of Power Development

The preceding remarks have contained repeated oblique reference to the scale or pace of power development, for in the last analysis this is the crucial issue in determining the nature of the power installation and the energy source used. A fundamental dictum of power economics is: the larger the plant the greater must be its utilization in order to obtain full advantage of the economy of scale. For that matter, any central-station generation with a distributive network provides the lowest cost power when the utilization factor is high and the distribution is over limited distances. Thus, the provision of central-station generation on any scale is difficult in the underdeveloped country, with its light and scattered loads. It has been pointed out that factors of 40 per cent or more can be obtained in the highly industrialized country where there are many factories, some of which may work more than one shift a day. In contrast, day work only is apt to be the rule in the industrial establishment in the underdeveloped country. Under these circumstances load factors of 20 to 25 per cent are more common.[20] In fact, any use of the central station for domestic or agricultural use will contribute to a low utilization factor.

Hydropower, with its very high capital costs (and now nuclear power as well) thus poses a dilemma. It offers the opportunity to install hydro capacity to serve a good industrial load of an energy-intensive activity, though this, as mentioned earlier, is not likely to contribute much to general economic development. But, to the extent that surplus power beyond the industrial need is distributed to the countryside, the light load will mean high unit costs.

Hubbard has suggested that in view of the special advantage this gives diesel generation, steam central stations should be built only when the maximum load is more than 10,000 kw. At lower levels it is preferable to build a small network of diesel plants of 1,000–1,500 kw capacity.[21] There is much merit in this approach, but the following kind of argument must be answered: "the annual payment for imported fuel oil consumed in a steam-plant operating at a high load-factor would be equal in amount to the annual charges on a loan to finance the importation of all of the equipment for a hydro-electric development whose generating capacity would be six to eight times greater than the capacity of the steam plant. Thus, if payments overseas are regarded as a limiting factor, it may be better to develop a hydro-electric station with a high capital cost than a steam station."[22]

In reply, note first that the greater capacity of the hydro project would presumably be excessive for a certain time and that this excess capacity would mean a higher cost for the power, and second that savings in the capital charges versus the fuel bill hold good only if the capital can be obtained. Once again, it is the provision of capital that is the great stumbling block.

Where does this leave us? There is, of course, no universal rule that one can apply in determining the appropriate size of plant and the pace of addition to capacity. Yet there is a way out of what seems to be very much a chicken-egg proposition. The most important prerequisite to electrification is higher income levels, with a greater consumer demand for goods and services of all sorts. As we know, the higher the income and the greater the consumer demand, the easier it is for the development process to take care of itself. The old adage "to him who hath shall be given" is dishearteningly apt here; the benefits of electric power are most easily and fully realized in an advanced economy.

Therefore, two rules are proposed: first, power capacity should be installed with the prime purpose of increasing per capita income and creating consumer demand; and second, in the presence of a subsistence income and an absence of consumer demand, power installation should be limited to the small and very small scale.

In other words, the author favors the small, isolated diesel generation approach, with the installation of thermal central stations and hydro projects only as the general base of power demand grows and can sustain the cost of distribution and transmission networks. This means an abandonment of the preoccupation with hydro and the assumption that power-intensive industry provides the basis for further economic development (although not the total abandonment of hydro development). It also means acknowledgement of the facts that the mere provision of power will *not* cause initial income growth, and that the best time to provide power is when it can be put to use, when its benefits can clearly be foreseen and identified, and not before.

The world needs electrification, to be sure, but let us not forget that it should be undertaken through a balanced approach, just as TVA itself was a balanced approach. The potential of power as a contribution to economic development and growth remains great, but it should not be exaggerated; nor should power development be engaged in with blind faith as a hopeful gamble. Properly applied, power development *can* aid in solving the problems of the underdeveloped regions and countries, and properly applied, it *will* do so.

References

1. Philip Sporn, in U. S. Congress, Joint Economic Committee, Subcommittee on Automation and Energy Resources, *Hearings, Energy Resources and Technology,* 86th Cong., 1st Sess., 1959, p. 51.
2. S. H. Schurr, "Energy," *Technology and Economic Development* (New York: Alfred A. Knopf, 1963), p. 75.
3. H. F. Mueller, "Problems of Energy Supply in Under-developed Countries with Special Regard to New Sources of Energy," *New Sources of Energy* (E/Conf. 35/2) (New York: United Nations, 1963), I, p. 79.

4. J. Stanovnik, "Power as a Factor of Development of Underdeveloped Coutries," World Power Conference, Sectional Meeting XI, Belgrade, 1957. Paper. Section A-B5 [Beograd, 1957] Vol. II, p. xiv.
5. M. Kahn, "Economic Importance of Integrated Utilization of Water Resources in Under-developed Countries," *ibid.,* p. 519.
6. Sporn, *op. cit.*, pp. 50 f.
7. Cf. United Nations, *Scientific Conference on The Conservation & Utilization of Resources 1949* (E/Conf. 7/7) (New York: United Nations, 1950), I, 207.
8. *Annual Report of the Tennessee Valley Authority* (Knoxville: Tennessee Valley Authority, 1959), p. 88.
9. S. H. Schurr, B. C. Netschert, *et al., Energy in the American Economy, 1850–1975* (Baltimore: Johns Hopkins University Press, 1960), pp. 188 f.
10. G. H. Daniel and E. A. F. Robinson, "Planning of Investment in Fuel and Power in Underdeveloped Countries," World Power Conference, *op. cit.,* p. 227.
11. Cf. F. Biaggi, F. Boselli, and P. Frossi, "Rapport entre les immobolisations de capital dans l'industrie manufacturiere et la puissance generatrice alimentant cette industrie," *ibid.,* pp. 585–620.
12. U. S., *Congressional Record*, 73d Cong., 1st Sess., 1933, v.77, pt. 2, p. 1423.
13. Cf. this statement: "Electric power tends to have a multiplier effect on economic development. Even the more extensive use of lighting and small motors, for instance, often increases the productivity of handicraft and small scale industry in ways which cannot be measured in advance." (W. L. Cisler, F. D. Campbell, and G. H. Craig, "Optimum Investment in Electric Power for Economically Underdeveloped Countries," World Power Conference, *op. cit.,* p. 321.)
14. M. de Verteuil and J. Ribadeau-Dumas, "Utilization de l'energie disponible d'une chute d'eau pour le traitement de l'aluminum en Afrique Centrale," *ibid.,* pp. 479–489.
15. Kahn, *op. cit.,* p. 521.
16. Hong Wong, discussion remarks, *ibid.,* p. 808.
17. Sporn, *op. cit.,* p. 52.
18. M. E. Hubbard, "The Use of Oil in Developing Countries," World Power Conference, *op. cit.,* p. 287.
19. Cisler, *et al., op. cit.,* p. 314.
20. Hubbard, *op. cit.,* p. 285.
21. *Ibid.,* pp. 285, 287.
22. Daniel and Robinson, *op. cit.,* p. 233.

The Application of TVA Experience to Underdeveloped Countries

JOHN OLIVER graduated with a B.S. degree from Oklahoma A. & M. College and with a M.A. degree from the University of Chicago. Mr. Oliver was a member of the Budget Staff of TVA from 1942 to 1946 and was Chief Budget Officer and Assistant General Manager from 1946 to 1951. From 1951 to 1954 he served as TVA's General Manager. During the period from 1954 to 1956 he was Assistant to the President of Wheland Company. Mr. Oliver is currently President of Development and Resources Corporation.

Some years ago, I accompanied the late Gordon Clapp, who was then chairman of the TVA, to a conference with an official in Washington on a matter of concern to the Tennessee Valley. Mr. Clapp presented our case with his usual frankness and conviction. At the conclusion of the meeting, as our host walked with us to the door—and possibly to add a note of warmth to what had been a fairly cool reception—he mentioned that his wife had been a native of Tennessee but that he had not been there in many years. I expressed the hope that he would soon correct that situation and while he was about it take a careful look at TVA. His response left no doubt as to how he felt about my suggestion. "I am not," he said, "one of those who feel that a first order of business is to drop whatever they are doing and run off to visit TVA." It was obvious that this particular individual had been hearing more about TVA than he wanted to hear.

I recite this bit of ancient history because the incident is the exception which proves the rule: everybody wants to see the TVA. The stream of visitors continues year after year. None come more eagerly than students, governmental officials, and others from abroad. They come with the belief that practices and techniques of resource development applied by TVA can be usefully applied in their own countries. Since the end of World War II over 30,000 aliens have visited TVA for periods ranging from one day to several weeks. One thousand have come as trainees for varying periods, not infrequently several months, and have had an opportunity for detailed observation of the work of those divisions in which they were particularly interested.

TVA has earned a reputation for sound work in many different disciplines, but it is TVA as a whole—the basic concept and philosophy of the program—that is the magnet which draws people here and inspires emulation in other lands. On every continent of the globe, and in at least a score of countries, projects patterned in some degree, at least, on TVA have been planned or started; and the initials "TVA" have become a generic term to represent any kind of comprehensive development program. We have all seen references to "a TVA on the Jordan," "India's

TVA," "a TVA for Southeast Asia," "The North of Scotland TVA," "Mexico's TVA," and so on. Now, TVA has many facets, and it means different things to different people. Here I should like to consider a few of the attributes which I, on the basis of my own particular experience, believe that a developmental program or agency should have if it is accurately to be considered a counterpart TVA.

Obviously, any such agency will have something to do with water and with soils. It will be involved with construction and operation of multipurpose dams. But a genuine counterpart will have more than these elements in common with the prototype.

For one thing, there will be a charter setting forth clearly the objectives to be achieved and the principles which are to govern organization and methods. The principle of integration—the interrelationship of people, resources, and disciplines—will be clearly recognized, both in the charter and in actual operation. Technicians of all sorts will be responsible to a single management; and management, before decisions are made, will have the benefit of advice from a wide variety of technical sources. In our counterpart TVA, planning and execution will go hand in hand, or rather, will be a continuum, and both will be the responsibility of the single management. The TVA principle of looking upon nature as a unity is well known—and hardly anyone quarrels with it any more. But a corollary principle—unity of management—may not be equally well appreciated. TVA's success is due in large measure to the fact that its management got an early, firm grip on the responsibilities assigned to it, and has never relaxed.

For a variety of reasons, these principles—unity of management and the relationship of planning to execution—so familiar to TVA people, are difficult to achieve in most underdeveloped areas. In these areas there is a shortage not only of technical skills but more critically of management skills. And there is a shortage of capital. As a result, the decision-making process tends to become diffused and actions are frequently taken on a piecemeal basis.

More often than not, local financial support must be augmented by loans or grants from the international finance agencies, by the U. S. aid programs, or by supplier-credit arrangements. Each of these sources of capital has its own rules and regulations which must be met before loans or grants are made available. Each has its own criteria for the evaluation of projects. The capital-short country or agency naturally looks for those projects or activities which are bankable or eligible for grants and so, to this extent at least, the power of decision as to what projects will go forward and in what sequence rests outside the agency and even outside the country. There is something to the old proverb that "he who pays the piper calls the tune."

Management of a development agency which is expected to bring about fundamental changes in a region must have leverage commensurate with its responsibility *and must not be afraid to use that leverage*. This sounds axiomatic, but it is in the nature of things that management of an agency established outside the regular departmental or ministerial pattern will constantly be confronted with proposals that its functions be carried out in a more "regular" manner and under "standard," or "regular" governmental procedures. Moreover, any agency actually bringing about fundamental change is bound to face opposition from forces with vested interests in the status quo. An effective management will not let the powers, authority, or leverage which have been given it wither from lack of exercise or be whittled away by too many compromises. Management must have wide-based support, but it will not try to win universal popularity by sacrifice of the objectives it was set up to achieve. It will reconcile itself to the fact that if it is really going to be instrumental in bringing about change, it will, from time to time, be involved in controversy.

In his book on TVA published in 1955, Gordon Clapp wrote, "TVA is controversial because it is consequential; let it become insignificant to the public interest, an agency of no particular account, and people will stop arguing about it."[1] When I first read that statement, I thought it a little extravagant, perhaps a reflection of some of the specific issues Mr. Clapp had battled over. But in the intervening years I have witnessed, in other settings, controversy surrounding achievement and have come to the conclusion that the statement may have wider application than to TVA.

Our counterpart TVA will be characterized by a particular philosophy and point of view. This philosophy acknowledges that the job is going to be long and hard, that patience as well as intelligence and industry are required to achieve results. The agency will be wise enough to know that technology is not enough and that what happens in its area of operation will depend in the final analysis *on actions of the people it tries to serve.* The most dismal failures in developmental schemes have been brought about because the people were not prepared to make proper use of new facilities made available to them. Unless people, rather than mortar, steel, and chemical fertilizers, are recognized as the most important ingredient of any development program, that program is going to fail.

Furthermore, the program will combine short-range projects with long-time activities: people need to have their hope and interest stimulated by relatively short-range projects when the results of more fundamental changes are necessarily slow in appearing. In addition, the program of our counterpart TVA will be on a sufficient scale to capture men's imaginations, and the people working in that program will have a sense of mission—a feeling that nothing else they could be doing would be of greater significance.

To be more specific, let us consider two developments with especially strong historical ties to TVA—the Cauca Valley Corporation in Colombia and the Khuzistan Water and Power Authority in Iran. In both of these developments, the act of Congress establishing TVA was used as a reference in the drafting of their basic charters; former TVA employees served as consultants in the development of organization structures and schemes of work; TVA technical publications have been used almost as textbooks; and TVA policies and procedures in personnel administration, procurement, finance, and other management areas have been carefully studied for adaptation to the local scene. In each of the countries involved, the work has been considered so successful that legislation has been enacted creating additional regional agencies modeled after the first one.

The Cauca Valley Corporation

The Cauca Valley of Colombia is an even more sharply distinct region than the Valley of the Tennessee. Surrounded by mountains whose altitude generally exceeds 10,000 feet, the Cauca Valley was, until recent decades, very much isolated from the rest of the country. It encompasses over a million acres of good flat land; water is plentiful and the climate is healthy. But until about thirty years ago, the principal activity was cattle raising, since cattle could walk out of the valley to the market. The advent of highways changed this picture, and today the region is not more than twenty-four hours by truck from all points of economic significance within Colombia, except for the Atlantic coastal area.

In Colombia, as in so many parts of the world, there has been a great movement of rural population to the cities. In the 1950's peasants from all over the country emigrated in great numbers to the valley, and especially to the major city of Cali. Cauca attained a population growth rate double Colombia's high average, and Cali has grown at a rate of over 8 per cent a year.

In the early 1950's a small group of able and progressive business leaders, concerned over a lagging agriculture and convinced that a special effort must be made to raise general living standards of the region, persuaded the government to invite David E. Lilienthal to visit the area. Some of these men had read about TVA and had been particularly impressed by Lilienthal's book, *Democracy on the March.*[2] Mr. Lilienthal went to Colombia in the spring of 1954 and, after studying the Cauca Valley, recommended the establishment of an agency similar to TVA. On the basis of his recommendation and the enthusiasm and initiative of the regional leadership, the government created, in October, 1954, the Autonomous Regional Corporation of the Cauca.

The objectives of the Cauca Valley Corporation (CVC) are to provide electric power, control floods, provide irrigation, reclaim and improve land, regulate water for public and industrial supply, promote soil conservation, encourage proper land use, stimulate mineral resource development, and encourage improvement of communications and transportation. The charter provides that the Corporation shall act as an autonomous, decentralized, and non-political body; apply modern methods of technology and business; and carry out its activities in such a way that they will serve as a demonstration and training program, not only for the immediate area but for other regions of the country. CVC is empowered to participate and invest in ventures in association with private enterprise.

In 1957 the government turned over to CVC its majority holding in a power generating company serving primarily the Cali area. As of that date, Cali had adequate power, but in other towns and in the rural areas supply was grossly inadequate. CVC's major effort, then, was to extend service throughout the region as a means of encouraging general development and of slowing down the rate of migration to Cali. By the end of 1964, a considerable portion of the rural area and all of the forty-two municipalities of the Cauca Valley were receiving CVC power. The system growth is high—about 16 per cent a year. This means more than doubling the system every five years.

CVC undertook, in 1957, construction of a flood-control and drainage project benefiting some 12,000 acres surrounding the city of Cali. This project made feasible large-scale housing developments, both public and private, to alleviate the critical housing situation in the burgeoning city. Also in 1957, CVC started a 25,000-acre irrigation and drainage project in the northern part of the valley. The area had excellent soils, but because of flooding and swampy conditions, it could only be used for pasture. With drainage and flood control, it can be converted to crop production.

Previous agricultural extension activities in the valley have been consolidated into one service under CVC direction. Emphasis has been on home economics and 4-H Club work, helping the relatively poor farmers to improve their diets and their homes. By the end of 1964, CVC completed detailed soils maps on the flat part of the valley, following up on preliminary work done by the

Food and Agriculture Organization of the United Nations. Work in forestry is being carried out in several small watersheds. CVC cooperates closely with the University del Valle and, with the U. N. Special Fund, is financing a project to strengthen the faculty in agricultural economics. It has participated in the promotion and establishment of a regional industrial and agricultural development bank.

CVC's Board of Directors consists of seven members, three of whom (the Minister of Development and the governors of the states of Valle and Cauca) are *ex officio*. Two private members are appointed by the President, and two are elected by bodies representing agricultural, industrial, commercial, and professional interests.

The charter from the central government is a strong one, but CVC undoubtedly would have been short lived except for the fact that a very competent and dedicated group of men were on its first Board of Directors and an able, sagacious, and patient but determined man was appointed executive director. Financial and other support which had been anticipated from the government was not at first forthcoming, and for a while, it was touch-and-go as to whether the agency would survive.

Recently, Dr. Bernardo Garces Cordoba, CVC's executive director, describing those early days, wrote, "This was indeed a difficult period: suffice it to say we were sustained only, on the one hand, by the ever-widening interest and allegiance of the local population, in a remarkable alliance of people from all walks of life: business leaders; labor; the church; the University; students; political leaders. On the other, by the unfailing and totally disinterested support and advice of Mr. Lilienthal. And here," Dr. Garces goes on, "I should mention the remarkable fact that we were kept going, insofar as finances are concerned, by a local Bank manager, proceeding on his own initiative, who authorized very substantial, permanent and constantly increasing overdrafts to an organization existing only on paper, without a single physical asset to its name."

The charter gives the board broad powers to approve and amend its budget and to order the disposition of funds and assets as it sees fit. Since, however, the national government made no direct appropriation to the Corporation until 1963, it has had to seek funds from a variety of sources. The World Bank has financed most of the power system. Other sources of funds include revenues from power sales, a special local tax on real estate, allocations from a state tax on alcoholic beverages, and some U. S. Public Law 480 funds. As long as CVC must look outside Colombia for most of the capital required for expansion, what it is able to do depends heavily on its powers of persuasion with the United States and international agencies; and its program is necessarily shaped to a great extent by the requirements of these agencies, which have set up patterns and procedures for application over much broader areas.

Despite its difficulties, CVC has survived and grown with stable management and stable policies, through the Rojas Pinilla regime, the revolution which overthrew him in 1957, the transitional military junta, and the regularly elected administrations which have followed. Its charter decrees that CVC shall be non-political, and it seems to have succeeded in keeping itself from becoming embroiled in politics. It tries to concentrate on its job of building a region. It is, I believe, a prime example of a case where much of the philosophy and many of the principles of TVA have taken solid root in a foreign land.

The Khuzistan Development Program

Now, let us jump to the other side of the world to an area that was the heart of the old Persian Empire. It is called Khuzistan, and it lies north of the Persian Gulf in southwest Iran. It covers an area of 58,000 square miles and has a population of about 2,500,000—roughly one-tenth of Iran's total area and one-eighth of the population. The region's history is rich. The biblical Elamites held sway there for 2,000 years. Cyrus, Darius, and Xerxes were among its ancient kings. Alexander the Great passed through on his search for other worlds to conquer. So did Tamerlane. Until the fourteenth or fifteenth century A.D., the irrigated Karun Valley flourished as the seat of a prosperous agriculture, but about this time it went into a long decline. Wars, invasion, political instability, and neglect of the irrigation works finally took their toll.

Early in the present century oil was discovered in Khuzistan, and Iran became the sixth largest petroleum producer in the world. Large refineries were constructed, and a net work of pipelines carried oil to the Persian Gulf for export. But despite this newly tapped source of wealth, the lives of the people remained relatively unchanged. Khuzistan was far from the capital in Tehran and across the high Zagros Mountains. For the average man, it remained one of the more impoverished and desolate parts of the country.

Immediately after World War II, Iran embarked on a Seven-Year Development Plan. The program suffered from political, financial, and other difficulties which beset the country in that troubled period, and the results were disappointing. But in the mid-fifties, with increasing income from the nationalized oil resources, the government launched a second Seven-Year Plan. Heading the Plan Organization at this time was an able and dynamic economist-banker by the name of Abol Hassan Ebtehaj. Late in 1955, Ebtehaj, with the blessing of the government, invited David E. Lilienthal and Gordon R. Clapp to visit Iran. When they arrived early in 1956, they were asked to prepare a comprehensive program for the integrated development of the region. It was explained to them, however, that Iran needed a great deal more than a planning report; an effective program *implementation* was needed. Lilienthal and Clapp were asked to commit themselves in advance to take responsibility for carrying out whatever specific projects they recommended which were undertaken by the government. Now Lilienthal and Clapp had just established a company to provide advisory services in the resource field (Development and Resources Corporation—D&R), but their staff facilities at this time consisted of two secretaries and an agreement by the author that he would go to work for the company the following month. Not much to start with. It was clear, however, that the key to development would lie in harnessing the rivers of the region for irrigation and for power. Lilienthal and Clapp had had some experience in controlling rivers and believed they could put together an organization to do the work. They agreed to conduct a two-year program of surveys and investigations leading to recommendations for an action program.

This two-year survey program was supposed to run until mid-1958, but Iran, all too accustomed to surveys and studies without effective follow-up, was impatient for action. In December, 1956, Development and Resources Corporation agreed to submit recommendations for specific projects as soon as it had a sound basis for doing so, without waiting for completion of the comprehensive report.

By mid-1957, our survey had confirmed our initial impression about the area's resources and possibilities—an unlimited amount of natural gas, almost completely unused; five rivers fed from mountain snows, with water enough to irrigate 2,500,000 acres of land, and with a hydroelectric potential in excess of six million kilowatts. Many of the soils in the southern part of the region were unsuitable for irrigation because of salinity and high ground water; but on the plains to the north, and in the mountain valleys, there were hundreds of thousands of acres of much better land.

In September, 1957, D&R submitted its recommendations for the first steps of a long-range development program. These included:

1. A high, thin arch dam on the Dez River for irrigation, power, and flood control. The site on the Dez was suggested as the place to begin a system which could ultimately comprise fourteen dams.

2. A 132-kilovolt transmission line from Abadan north to the provincial capital of Ahwaz to utilize idle capacity from a steam plant owned by the oil companies until power from the dam could be made available.

3. Formation of an agency to manage production and transmission of electrical energy for the region.

4. A 10,000-acre sugar cane plantation with a mill and refinery. Sugar cane had grown in Khuzistan hundreds of years before but had completely disappeared. Iran wanted to restore this crop in Khuzistan, and our studies indicated this to be feasible.

5. Basic agricultural ground work for future irrigation projects, including a program to test and demonstrate workable and economic ways to use chemical fertilizers to increase food and fiber production.

6. A polyvinyl chloride plant. This project was recommended as the first step in a comprehensive industrial complex based, in part, on natural gas.

The program was quickly approved, although, because of a shortage of funds, the polyvinyl chloride plant was later abandoned before construction was started. Work on the program began at once under arrangements previously agreed upon. These were simple and straightforward. D&R was to submit, along with its program recommendations, estimates of the funds required to carry them out. Upon approval of the estimates by Plan Organization, advances would be made to D&R, which was required to submit, every six months, a statement of expenditures made from the advance account certified to by an independent firm of public accountants.

Effective governmental action in Iran, as in many other countries, is hampered by an excess of red tape. Plan Organization staff members knew that it would be impossible to carry out a program within the regular governmental framework on the schedules agreed upon and under regular governmental methods and procedures.

The flexibility so essential to getting the job done was achieved through the contracts with D&R, which gave it wide latitude in carrying out the program. As agent for Plan Organization, D&R prepared designs, specifications, and invitations for bids; analyzed bids; awarded over 200 contracts (of which ten had a value in excess of $1,000,000 each); supervised construction; and disbursed funds both for its own force account work and for the work of construction contractors. The contractors were a truly international group, coming from Great Britain, Italy, Holland, France, Japan, the United States, West Germany, Sweden, and other countries. D&R's own forces were drawn from a dozen nationalities.

As the full dimensions of the task began to emerge, it was a temptation to build our thin ranks by means of a wholesale raid on the personnel of TVA, but here we ran into difficulty. TVA was most helpful in all ways it considered appropriate; but it made clear that despite the importance of our task and the good will still held for us, raiding the active ranks of TVA was out of bounds. I believe TVA would agree we behaved in a reasonably decent fashion. We did employ a few people directly, but many more ex-TVA people came from other jobs. Over the past eight years, we have had approximately 400 different non-Iranian employees on Khuzistan work. Of this number, about half have been Americans, and of these, well over thirty have had TVA experience.

Today, the initial program recommended in 1957 is essentially complete. The dam, named in honor of the Shah, is in operation with 130,000 kw installed out of an ultimate capacity of 520,000 kw. It is a thin-arch structure towering 646 feet high in a spectacular gorge on the Dez River. Electricity consumption in the provincial capital of Ahwaz and the neighboring villages has increased 300 per cent since 1958, when the transmission line was completed from Abadan. Power from the dam also serves other cities of the region, recently connected to the new transmission network from Pahlavi Dam to Abadan/Khorramshahr.

Controlled flow of water from Dez reservoir has been brought to a 50,000-acre pilot irrigation area, where farmers are learning improved agricultural practices, the value of fertilizers and improved seed varieties, and the most effective use of irrigation water. In the pilot irrigation project, the desert truly has been made to bloom; and during the next four years, the irrigation network will be expanded to bring controlled flow of water to 360,000 acres. Additionally, the sugar cane project has been through three commercial harvests; and sugar cane, after a lapse of several hundred years, has been re-established in one of the first areas in which it was ever cultivated.

The new physical works are impressive; so are the increases in agricultural production and use of electric energy. But as mentioned earlier in this discussion, people are the most important ingredient of a development program. If, when the foreign advisers, technicians, and managers depart, they do not leave behind them people who can successfully carry on what has been started, they might better have stayed home in the first place. Training of Iranians has therefore been a central objective from the beginning, training them in the wide variety of skills necessary in this complex operation: bulldozer operators, village agricultural workers, hot-line maintenance crews, and all the rest. Practical on-the-job training has been emphasized rather than formal course work.

In May, 1960, by an act of the Iranian Parliament, the Khuzistan Water and Power Authority was created to own and operate the facilities in the program. By a series of steps carefully developed, agreed to, and scheduled in advance, D&R began turning over to KWPA the managerial functions it had previously handled on behalf of Plan Organization. In June, 1963, D&R's role became that of general consultant. At the time of each step in the transfer process, D&R assigned to KWPA its overseas employees in the units being transferred—to work administratively for KWPA, but with D&R remaining responsible for the quality of their work. As qualified Iranians become available for managerial and technical posts held by D&R expatriates, they are assigned to these positions. At the present time, about seventy-five D&R employees remain on assignment to KWPA.

Each step in the process of transfer was developed most carefully with the managing director of KWPA, H. E. Abdol Reza Ansari, because we all believed this to be one of the most delicate phases of the whole program. The criterion for selection of D&R employees in the beginning was whether they could get jobs done, not their skill in working themselves out of jobs. It is not easy for a line supervisor to step aside into a supporting role, or to submit actions for the approval of a man he once trained and supervised. As for new KWPA personnel, many of those with good theoretical training lacked practical operating experience. Some were eager for title and office without full appreciation of the concomitant responsibility. The process of takeover began during a period of heightened nationalistic feeling in the country at large, when the idea of getting rid of all foreign advisors and consultants was a popular one. Some politicians had tried to make capital out of the heavy delegations made by Plan Organization to D&R, a foreign concern, in the handling of Iran's money. There were all sorts of opportunities for friction and misunderstandings which could have left matters in a shambles.

The program was most fortunate, however, in the caliber of the KWPA managing director and the deputies he selected around which to build his permanent organization. They have approached their responsibilities soberly and with keen understanding of the psychological hazards involved in the transfer. The process has gone well. There have been touchy moments but never loss of confidence that our objectives are truly identical: the building of an Iranian institution which can, without loss of momentum, carry on the work in Khuzistan with a minimum of outside assistance. To date, Iran has invested over $190 million in the program. Except for a $42 million loan from the World Bank, the funds have come from Iran's oil revenues. No United States aid or other grant funds have gone into the program.

Accurate statistics are sometimes difficult to find in Iran, and we have no single measure of the effect of the program upon the economy of the region and the income of the people. But precise statistics are not necessary for one to be convinced that there has been a change. The city of Ahwaz, where the impact of the program was first felt, has a different look about it. It shows unmistakable signs of rapid growth and change. It is cleaner; the shops and bazaars have been dressed up; there is a greater variety of goods for sale. Similar changes are beginning to take place in Andimeshk and in the ancient city of Dezful. Employment on the sugar plantation at Haft Tapeh, near the ruins of ancient Susa, is putting cash and purchasing power into an area which had very little of either before. In the seventeen villages of the Pilot Irrigation Project, the villagers are buying more shoes, more bicycles, and more radios. Their diet is improving. So is their health.

Of equal significance, however, are evidences of a new feeling of confidence on the part of the people. Iranians are accustomed to hearing about great schemes, many of which never get out of the talking stage. Consequently, in the beginning, there was a great amount of cynicism about the Khuzistan program. When plans for the dam and sugar cane factory were announced, only a small minority thought they would actually be built. Once started, many believed that the projects would never be finished. Once finished, it was assumed they probably wouldn't work. But as predictions, one after another, have come to pass, the old spirit of pessimism and cynicism has begun to fade. There is now new hope for a better future in Khuzistan.

Conclusion

Over thirty years ago the United States broke with tradition and established the TVA, its first regional agency for economic development. Part of the worldwide interest illustrated by the cases of the Cauca Valley and Khuzistan springs from a recognition in the less developed nations of their need, even greater than that of the United States, to break with the traditional forms of government administration in order to cope with modern problems of resource development and administration. In the United States, TVA grew in part from a feeling that in this type of activity, centralization of federal power in Washington should be reduced and the powers of the states preserved. In many less developed countries the central power is the only real power. Its administration is bound by the traditions of the past. But the eyes of the people are fixed more and more on the opportunities of the future, and wise leadership is searching for means to break with the past and move toward the future. The TVA example has proved helpful.

References

1. Gordon R. Clapp, *The TVA: An Approach to the Development of a Region* (Chicago: University of Chicago Press, 1955), p. 3.
2. David E. Lilienthal, *TVA: Democracy on the March* (New York: Harper & Brothers, 1944).

Natural Resource Problems and TVA

JOSEPH L. FISHER is a graduate of Bowdoin College and holds the M.A. and Ph.D. degrees from Harvard. Dr. Fisher was Executive Officer of the Council of Economic Advisers from 1947 to 1953 and Associate Director of Resources for the Future from 1953 to 1959. Since 1959 he has been President of Resources for the Future. He is the co-author of *Resources in America's Future.*

Thirty years and a little more have passed since the New Deal began—nearly a third of a century. These three decades have been epochal in our national history. We have passed through the Great Depression and the second and greatest world war, and we are still living in a protracted uncertain cold war. The development of less developed countries has become the concern of all. On the domestic side, we seem to have learned how to avoid the catastrophe of major depression, but we have not discovered the secret of sustained high-level employment and economic activity. The goal of no more than 3 per cent of the labor force unemployed on the average has turned out to be an elusive one. At least one-fifth of our people are genuinely poor. Perhaps as many are poorly educated by any acceptable standard.

The Tennessee Valley has shared in the ups and downs of the national economy during these years and has been buffeted by the same national and international forces; and although significant gains have been made, this valley in the heart of the southeastern United States has remained somewhat worse off than the country as a whole according to most measures of economic welfare.

The most distinguishing feature of the Tennessee Valley during the past three decades has been the Tennessee Valley Authority, a bold experiment in regional resource development now widely known over the whole world. In economic and social terms other parts of the Southeast are similar to the Tennessee Valley except that they have no regional authority.

An attempt to appraise the impact of TVA after thirty years of history is probably inevitable. If TVA were a man, it would now be coming into the fullness of its powers, into adult maturity, ready to make its largest contributions. Is TVA now, or likely soon to be, on such a threshold—or are its greatest days already behind it with nothing ahead but the playing out of music already composed?

I am not the one to appraise the economic impact of TVA on the people of this region, the Southeast, the nation, or the world. This is better left to those who know first-hand about TVA.

(When I left graduate school in 1938 looking for a job, I applied to TVA and received an "if offered would you accept?" telegram concerning a position, I think, in the transportation division. Unfortunately, in the meantime I had accepted a teaching position, so I missed my opportunity to join the TVA family and learn about it from the inside.) What I shall try to do instead is call attention to a number of economic and related trends that are moving strongly in this country, project them a little distance into the future, and raise certain questions as to what these trends may mean for the TVA of the future. The answers will have to be provided by the people in TVA and in the Tennessee Valley. The several trends I shall cite are well known, but I shall try to pick out of them a few elements that will be of interest in the context of regional development problems.

Urban Growth and Natural Resources

The tendency of cities to grow in population faster than the nation as a whole has been marked for many decades past. In this country 70 or more per cent of the people now live in urban areas and the end of this movement is yet some time ahead of us. In the Tennessee Valley the percentage is lower, but the tendency toward urban living here has also been striking. The farm population of the country has been cut in half since the war, and some think that it may be cut in half again before this tendency has played itself out; the same trend may be observed in the Tennessee Valley region. Many of the individuals and families leaving farms have gone to nearby towns and cities; many have also moved a greater distance to the major metropolitan areas of the North and West.

By the year 2000, when we shall most likely have a population exceeding 300 million—perhaps around 330 million—we can expect the entire increase in population of about 150 million to live in urban areas. Even those who will continue to engage in agriculture may well choose to live in cities and commute to their farms.

What will demographic trends such as these mean for a regional development agency that historically has been oriented to natural resources and the rural scene—to improving agriculture and forestry, to building dams and transmission lines for electric power, to providing reservoirs and outdoor recreation? This is not to say that TVA has not already had extensive and useful relations with city planning agencies, municipal government, and other urban activities; it is rather to raise the question of whether these relations may not have to be intensified in the future and given new directions and form. The planning and development of metropolitan regions is tending to become one and the same problem with planning and development of large natural-resource regions.

Rising Levels of Living and Outdoor Recreation

In a recent study undertaken by Resources for the Future, we tried to project the general size and shape of the American economy to 1980 and 2000. We estimated that a growing labor force working with increasing productivity could produce a total national product in 1980 of about twice that of 1960, and by the year 2000 nearly four-and-a-half times as large.[1] These estimates imply an annual rate of growth in the gross national product of about 3.8 per cent. Accompanying this large growth of production would be a similarly large growth in personal consumption expenditures with per capita purchases increasing from $1,830 in 1960 to $2,700 in 1980 and about $4,000 in 2000. If the national economy is able to grow by 5 per cent a year, which is the target set by many persons, because of higher rates of productivity, then per capita purchases would increase at a rate one-third higher.

The national economy, growing in this manner, would provide much larger markets for most goods and services. If past trends hold, we may expect the demand for services as a category to increase more rapidly than the demand for agricultural or industrial production. More transportation, education, medical services, and outdoor recreation will be required.

TVA is concerned with providing a number of services; let me discuss briefly the future prospects for one of them, outdoor recreation. For some years past, the use of land and water areas for outdoor recreation has been increasing very rapidly.[2] Annual visits to TVA reservoirs have increased at more or less the same rate as the other areas, perhaps a little faster. The factors behind this rapid growth have been expanding population, rising incomes, added leisure time with a shorter work week and longer summer vacations, increased mobility as the family automobile has become common, and perhaps a more intense desire for people to escape the humdrum of office and factory work.

In the long-range estimates cited earlier, we in Resources for the Future projected a rate of growth in use and demand for outdoor recreation as far ahead as 1980 and 2000, largely on the basis of past trends in these factors, and we came up with an average annual increase of 6 to 8 per cent for the decades to the end of the century, depending on the type of area. However one looks at it, the increases are likely to be tremendous and will tax the capacity of public and private agencies. Depending upon the intensity of use in terms of visits per acre, for example, many additional acres of recreation land might be needed. The use that can be supported comfortably will depend on the design and arrangement of the facilities and on use patterns. But putting all of these factors together in as reasonable a way as we could, we came to the conclusion that perhaps twice as many acres in national parks would be needed by 2000 and perhaps three or four times as much recreation area within national forests. Quite likely, even larger increases in state parks will be desirable since state parks can provide the much-needed intermediate type of outdoor recreation lying within a few hours' drive of major concentrations of population.

Outdoor recreation is one of the rapid growth industries of the country. Has TVA, as well as many other agencies concerned with this industry, fully appreciated the magnitude of growth that is in prospect, and are the plans sufficiently ambitious?

Changing Demands for Natural Resource Products

In our book, *Resources in America's Future*, we went to some pains to project the demand for a large number of raw materials and resource products over the balance of this country. Beginning with projections of the general size and shape of the economy based on assumptions regarding population, labor force, and productivity, we proceeded to make estimates of the amount of final consumer goods and services that would be required to match up with over-all capacity. Included were estimates of food requirements, housing, heat and power, and many others. New technology, as best we could foresee its application, was considered in making the estimates, as was the possibility of export and import of materials. Changes in taste and in demand generally arising from increasing incomes were dealt with systematically. The most artificial feature of the projections was the assumption that relative prices of the various materials would not change. This assumption, by allowing gaps to open between demand and supply, made it possible to see clearly where the problems of deficiency and of oversupply are likely to arise, thus pointing the way for public and private policies and actions to do something about the imbalances.

One of the most interesting sets of projections is that for the energy commodities. Historically, demand for energy in all its uses has for several decades been growing more slowly than has the total national production; we assumed this relationship would hold for the next several decades. The absolute demand for the major energy commodities, as we projected them, increases, although much more slowly for coal than for the others. In 1960, coal furnished about 25 per cent of the total energy supply; by 1980 we estimated that this would fall to 20 per cent and by 2000, to 13 per cent. The demand for oil we expect to remain more or less the same, at about 40 per cent of total supply, while the demand for natural gas may subside slightly after 1980. Hydropower in 1960 was approximately 3.6 per cent of the total; this may diminish slightly by 1980 and somewhat more sharply thereafter, to an estimated 2 per cent in 2000. Nuclear energy, principally for electric power generation, was hardly visible in 1960, but by 1980 we anticipate nearly 5 per cent of the total energy supply will come from nuclear sources and by 2000, nearly 15 per cent. This, of course, assumes further reductions in the cost of nuclear power, for which recent signs have been hopeful. It is quite likely that costs of producing electric power from more conventional sources will also decrease; thus, it is clear that nuclear costs must meet this added challenge if this source of power is to become a prominent part of the picture. By the year 2000 we anticipate that as much as half of all electricity will be derived from nuclear processes, and that a considerably higher portion of the newly installed generating facilities at that time will be nuclear. It has to be kept in mind that electricity in 1960 made up only about 20 per cent of all energy consumption. This we anticipate will rise to about 27 or 28 per cent by the year 2000. As things now look, principal competitors in producing electricity in the later years of the century, if not sooner, will be the atom and coal.

A few words about technological possibilities may be enlightening. To begin with, in the case of coal, if there were to be no further increase in efficiency of use between now and the year 2000, the nation would require on the order of 30 per cent more coal in that year—nearly 200 million tons—than it would assuming a continuation of technical improvements. If coal should lose additional amounts of the steam boiler market to nuclear energy over the next thirty or forty years, what are some of the technological possibilities that might work to the advantage of coal? One of the "farther-out" possibilities would be the improvement in wide-scale application of the fuel cell to power vehicles, assuming that the hydrogen, or perhaps other fuel, used in the cell could be derived more cheaply from coal than from any alternative raw material. Other possibilities include lower cost transportation of coal in slurry form through pipelines, further changes in industrial location which would make possible much more use of coal at the mine to produce electric power or for use as process heat in industrial operations, underground gasification of coal, and cheap production of liquid fuel from coal.

A similar story could be recited for the other major energy commodities. Oil presents a most interesting case. In addition to the likelihood of further discoveries in this country, although probably on a more modest scale than in the past, there are yet unexploited possibilities for secondary recovery from existing wells. Immense reserves of oil shale exist in the western states, and recent estimates based on pilot-plant operations indicate that gasoline and other products can be extracted from the hard shale at a cost only marginally above that from the conventional underground liquid sources. Beyond this are the equally large reserves of oil in the so-called tar sands of the prairie provinces in Canada. Looking abroad to the Middle East, Venezuela, and North Africa, one finds very large reserves already discovered and known to be economic, plus inferred reserves much larger still. The world oil outlook has shifted dramatically since the war from one of possible shortage, rising costs, and prices, and difficulty generally, to one of probable oversupply and even glut on the world markets for some years to come. Indeed, this country undoubtedly would import a much higher proportion of its total supply than the 17 or so per cent of recent years, except for quotas set on imports. The energy commodities for the most part enter substantially into world trade, the notable exception being natural gas, and even this may have a considerable future in international trade with the perfection of tankers to carry gas in liquid form at very low temperatures. Therefore, costs of production in various parts of the world, world prices, improvements in transportation, and tariff and other trade regulations applied by different nations and groups of nations all become important for every part of the world that is involved in the pattern of world energy.

The TVA region has been blessed by good hydroelectric sites and by nearness to cheap coal. It has also been called upon to supply a large amount of electric power to the national atomic-energy program. What are the trends and visible possibilities on a national and world scale in energy that will be significant to the Tennessee Valley and to TVA? Many moves and countermoves exist as possibilities on the chess board of world energy demand and supply involving new technology, changes in demand, and political events at home and elsewhere in the world.

In our study of resources in this country, we also examined the prospects for agricultural products, fertilizers, forest products, water, and the rest. I shall make only a few comments here. In agriculture we anticipate very little change in the requirement for acres of farm land. A much larger population living at somewhat higher standards regarding food, we concluded, can be accommodated from the same number of acres with technical improvements in agriculture continuing to substitute for what otherwise would be an increased demand for land itself. As in the past, this is quite largely a story of more fertilizers more skillfully applied. The contributions of TVA in the past are well known; they will have to be no less in the future if our rather optimistic outlook for agriculture is to be realized.

For forest products, we were inclined to see some considerable difficulty of supply toward the end of this century—unless we were to take the improvident step of reducing our growing stock to a dangerous level, in which case even greater difficulty would soon follow. It is possible that we underestimated further improvements in silviculture and in the technology of wood processing and use. We may also have underestimated the possibilities for reducing losses due to insects, diseases, and fire. Our rather pessimistic outlook in forest products has been challenged by people in the industry; however, it has been more or less in line with the longer range outlook suggested by the U. S. Forest Service. If this outlook is the correct one, then it argues for increased attention to our forest resources all along the line. The elusive potential of small ownerships in the southeastern part of the country for producing more usable timber products is well known. TVA has been trying, with some success, to get at this problem, but there is a long way to go in institutional and other improvements if this potential is more nearly to be realized.

Only a few words on the outlook for water resources: in the East, the biggest problem by far would appear to be one of maintaining quality and managing whole river systems for quality purposes. This is not to say that the more conventional uses of water will not be important—navigation, flood control, hydroelectric power generation—but that the overriding problem is likely to be quality. Quality standards are important, not only for domestic consumption of water but also for industrial uses, many of which now will not tolerate impurities, and for recreation uses. Furthermore, much of the additional water storage capacity in the eastern states will have as its chief purpose the maintenance of flow at times of low flow in order to move pollutants downstream and into the ocean. Whole rivers, such as the Potomac, are going to have to be dealt with systematically if efficient quality control is to be achieved. Alternative ways of reducing and preventing pollution will have to be embraced by the analysis, including flow maintenance, treatment in various ways, and recycling in particular uses. Costs of achieving designated levels of water purity on specific stretches of a stream need to be estimated so that least-cost programs can be decided on. The powerful and fascinating apparatus of systems analysis can be applied to these matters to improve decisions by public and private agencies.[3]

In the West, not counting the Pacific Northwest where the water supplies are relatively plentiful, scarcity presents certain problems. The chief one seems to be that of an orderly transition from using water primarily for irrigation farming, frequently to produce crops already in surplus, to using more of the limited supply for industrial, recreation, and domestic purposes. This transition will be essential for further population and economic growth in many of the arid parts of the country. In one recent study it was estimated that new water supply in New Mexico would increase the state income some fifty times as much if used in industry rather than for irrigation.[4] Investigations of the legal and economic impediments to this transition are now being undertaken in some depth.[5]

River basins in the humid East do not face the difficulties of major shift in water use in the dramatic way the western states do, but the lesson is clear: in every part of the country water should be allocated to the higher value uses, counting social values as well as market values, to the point where marginal returns net of costs are equal in the various uses. TVA will want to keep up on changes in value of water for the several purposes—recreation, industrial use, flood control, navigation, hydropower—so that it can foresee the changes and encourage timely adjustments. River-system management for quality control will also become of increasing importance here as more water-using and water-polluting industries are established in the Valley and as more people come here for recreation at the reservoirs and along the streams.

Chronic Unemployment and Poverty

The national spotlight is now focused on poverty and on the Appalachian region of high unemployment. The richest, most productive national economy in all history has not erased poverty and unemployment everywhere within its borders. In the Tennessee Valley region and the Southeast generally, economic development has been catching up with the country as a whole during the past thirty years. Prior to TVA, in 1929, per capita income in the Valley was $317, only 45 per cent of the national average. By 1960 per capita income had reached $1,378 or 64 per cent of the national average.[6] There is still quite a distance to go. The eastern part of the Tennessee Valley is a part of Appalachia and shares the problems of that region. Agricultural employment over the entire valley still forms a significantly higher percentage of total employment than in the nation as a whole. Much of the Valley's agriculture is subsistence farming. Many of the forest holdings are small and do not lend themselves readily to efficient forestry. Forest industry employment tends to be low paid. The textile industry is not a rapid-growth industry, especially that portion based on natural fibers. Migration from the Valley, as from the Southeast, has continued and has reduced what otherwise would have been a much more severe problem of unemployment. All of this is the familiar story of chronic difficulty only partially offset by out-migration and new manufacturing and service industry development. I don't mean to exaggerate this set of problems: the Valley region has made good headway in meeting them. But, as I read the trends, more strenuous efforts still are needed before this region will catch up with national averages of material welfare or will find itself riding the middle of the business cycle instead of the side of high unemployment.

One hopes the Johnson administration's antipoverty war and

the program for Appalachia will succeed in reducing chronic unemployment. Especially, one hopes it will be possible to encourage on a selective basis even faster out-migration, as well as educational, training, and industrial development programs within the problem area. What will be TVA's stance on these matters? How will it gear its own regional programs to mesh with these new national ones? What can the national program for Appalachia and the national poverty program learn from the TVA experience?

Regional Development Concepts and TVA

TVA means something in this country and in the world. John F. Kennedy was right when he said in 1963, "in the minds of men the world over, the initials TVA stand for progress." In my view, most important are the ideas TVA has come to signify, such as the idea of regional development with the regional agency of the national government leading and encouraging numerous public and private agencies within the region to improve the lot of the people living there. TVA signifies also an analytical approach to regional problems, in which various parts are interrelated and on the basis of which corrective programs of a multipurpose nature are designed and put into effect. Standing at the center have been the control and development of the river for flood control, navigation, and electric power primarily, but also for outdoor recreation, industry, domestic water supply, and other purposes.

The purposes of regional economic development have been stated in various ways: to reach or surpass the level of national development, to achieve a more balanced growth which usually is thought to mean more industry, to correct chronic problems of high unemployment or instability, or more vaguely to realize the region's development potentialities. Natural resources development is beneficial only as it enables these purposes to be fulfilled. But the purposes themselves continually need redefinition and clarification. Fortunately, recent advances in analytical techniques, many of them statistical, such as regional input-output and systems analysis, now make it possible to think more precisely and operationally on these matters. Regional agencies will want to make use of these techniques and apply and improve them.[7]

The country abounds in regional resource planning efforts, but except perhaps for TVA each is concerned with one or at most a few particular activities. One cannot help but wonder why TVA, admittedly now a huge success in its own region, has not been imitated elsewhere in this country; in other parts of the world it has been the inspiration for a number of valley development schemes. Was TVA unique to the economic, social, and political situation of the Great Depression in this country? Have events moved forward so rapidly that the geographic scale of the TVA operation is now too small? Have the states outside the Tennessee Valley seen in TVA, if it should be repeated or adapted in other parts of the country, a threat to themselves so substantial that political support for additional TVA's cannot be found? Or has the TVA devotion to working with states and localities been so successful and strengthened them so much that the establishment of other regional resource authorities does not seem necessary any longer? Has there been some deficiency at the conceptual and adminstrative levels, such as an inability to deal in a constructive and sustained way with the whole range of social and economic problems of a region? Has there been a tendency to narrow and concentrate more and more on the development and use of a river and on providing electric power at the loss of intellectual excitement that comes with a broader range of concerns? These are interesting questions which have to be addressed in any effort to appraise TVA against the sweep of history over the past several decades.

It may be that TVA was one particular kind of program in response to the problems of a particular valley at a particular time, and that since then other responses to substantially the same set of conditions have appeared and been tried: the interagency river-basin commissions in the Southeast and in Texas, for example; or the new and promising federal-state compact for the Delaware River; or the interagency arrangements in several of the large western river basins; or the leadership of a single state of its water development, as in California. My own preference is for experimentation with a variety of administrative forms as we have been doing in recent years. Possibly one or two of these should be more closely modeled on TVA. At one time, I thought the Columbia River Basin would be a good candidate for a federal regional river authority. I remember working on a bill and presidential message on this subject in the late 1940's in the executive offices of the President, but it did not carry far despite what seemed to me at the time compelling arguments for it. Perhaps the looser arrangements found in other river basins, by arousing less political opposition, can, over time, accomplish as much in integrated resource development and involve more units of government in a directly participating way. Certainly federal paternalism would be less, but the difficulties of strong and continuous leadership from the center would be greater.

Concluding Observations

It is not easy to appraise the trends in administrative theory and practice, let alone intellectual trends, relevant to the evaluation of TVA. Perhaps this is a proper note of uncertainty and questioning with which to end these remarks. But I cannot refrain from adding a few concluding observations. It is customary in symposia oriented to organizations or movements not already dead to say that they stand at a crossroads, that their best years lie ahead, that moments for great decisions are at hand. I don't know if such things should now be said about TVA, although I suspect they apply today to any group still on its toes and looking ahead.

I have tried to call attention to several economic and related trends which I believe to be moving rather powerfully in this country and which a regional resource development agency obviously must take account of. For several of these—such as the increasing demand for outdoor recreation, the deepening problem of water pollution, the shifting sources and uses of energy commodities, the movement of people out of agriculture, and the growth of urban areas—I have drawn especially from the findings of research undertaken by Resources for the Future. In each case I have ended, not with advice for TVA, but with a question or two for further consideration. Perhaps more than anything else the vitality of a regional agency, program, movement, and idea depends on a genuine confrontation of the right questions. Standing between the national interest on the one hand and state and local interests on the other, the regional agency inevitably must carry water on both shoulders. It has to discharge responsibilities in two directions. But more than this it has a positive, creative role to play. TVA over a span of thirty years has developed and applied the concepts of integrated river and resource programs for the benefit of all the people in its region. Its place in history is secure. Can as much be said regarding its future?

References

1. Hans H. Landsberg, Leonard L. Fischman, and Joseph L. Fisher, *Resources in America's Future* (Baltimore: Johns Hopkins University Press, 1963).
2. Marion Clawson, *Statistics on Outdoor Recreation* (Baltimore: Johns Hopkins University Press, 1958).
3. Allen V. Kneese, *Water Pollution—Economic Aspects and Research Needs* (Baltimore: Johns Hopkins University Press, 1962); Allen V. Kneese, *The Economics of Regional Water Quality Management* (Baltimore: Johns Hopkins University Press, 1964); and Arthur Maass *et al.*, *Design of Water-Resource Systems* (Cambridge, Mass.: Harvard University Press, 1962).
4. Nathaniel Wollman, *The Value of Water in Alternative Uses* (Albuquerque: University of New Mexico Press, 1962).
5. L. M. Hartmen and D. A. Seastone at Colorado State University.
6. Stefan Robock, "Integrated River-Basin Development and Industrialization: The Tennessee Valley Experience," in *Science, Technology, and Development; United States Papers Prepared for the United Nations Conference on Application of Science and Technology for Benefit of Less Developed Areas*, Volume IV, *Industrial Development* (Washington: U. S. Government Printing Office, 1962–63). 12 v.
7. Werner Hochwald, ed., *Design of Regional Accounts* (Baltimore: Johns Hopkins University Press, 1961); and Werner Hirsch, ed., *Elements of Regional Accounts* (Baltimore: Johns Hopkins University Press, 1964).

The Politics of Water Resource Development as Exemplified by TVA

NORMAN WENGERT earned A.B., LL.B., and Ph.D. degrees from the University of Wisconsin and the A.M. degree from Fletcher School of Law and Diplomacy. He was employed by TVA from 1941 to 1948. He then held various positions in teaching, research, and government before becoming Professor of Public Administration at Maryland in 1955. In 1960 he assumed his present duties as Professor and Head of the Department of Political Science at Wayne State University. Dr. Wengert is the author of *Valley of Tomorrow: TVA and Agriculture*; *Natural Resources and the Political Struggle*; and *India's Food Crisis and Steps to Meet It* (co-author).

It is hardly necessary to explain that TVA has been involved in politics. No other river in America has been more deeply involved in politics than the Tennessee River; no other water development program has aroused more political discussion than the program delegated to the Tennessee Valley Authority for execution. Anyone who has lived in the Valley, or who at one time or another has worked for TVA, knows the extent to which the three letters TVA have spelled politics.

The title of this article might perhaps be restated as "The Uses of Politics," or "What is the Good of Politics?" In seeking an answer to this question, insight may be gained into why TVA has been so deeply involved in politics, why over the past thirty years so many controversies have raged over the development of the Tennessee River. As some of the political woes (as well as victories) of TVA are recalled, perhaps they may suggest that such struggles represent a vital aspect of democracy in America.

But what is meant by the term "politics"? Unfortunately, this word has many meanings and connotations, reflecting a variety of attitudes and popular beliefs, as well as reflecting an area of technical study and research.

On the one hand, participation in politics is urged as a duty of citizenship. But on the other hand, in popular parlance, "politics" often connotates something bad, something distasteful, something with which most people would rather not be associated. Traditionally, political scientists have contributed to this hostility to politics by being in the forefront of movements which sought to "get politics out of government." (One such movement produced non-partisan city elections to combat what Lincoln Steffens had called "The Shame of the Cities.")

At the administrative level this hostility to politics is deeply imbedded in our civil service laws—for example, in the federal Hatch Act—and in the general stress on the neutrality of public employees. Among administrative agencies, stress on political neutrality has at times been related to endeavors to minimize legislative control and even to reduce public scrutiny, a frequent device being to provide for automatic or independent financing through dedicated taxes, special mileage rates, or authorizations to use revenue. But, efforts to remove governmental activities from politics to avoid corruption and to reduce controversy have rested on essentially negative conceptions of the nature and role of politics.

By the use of the term "politics" in this article a special and more focused meaning is suggested. It is applied as a general designation to the interactive processes by which governmental decisions are made. In this usage, both *process* and *decision* are stressed.

In a now classic phrase, Harold Lasswell suggested some thirty years ago that politics was concerned with "Who gets what, when, how?"[1] To traditional reformers of a progressive persuasion who looked primarily at the word "getting," this phrase sounded like the graft and corruption they were fighting, and perhaps it reinforced their zeal. When Lasswell wrote, few political scientists were ready to move beyond the term "getting" in his intriguing title, because they were still deeply enmeshed in governmental reform movements.

More recently, however, political scientists have begun to focus upon the government as a process,[2] looking at the "who," the "what," the "when," and the "how." The "who," of course, represents the actors in the decision process, the individuals and groups who identify problems and formulate issues for political decision. The "what" reflects the programmatic factors, what government does, that constitute one of the parameters within which action occurs. The "when" highlights the time dimension, since by definition decisions deal with the short- or long-range future. And finally, the "how" of Lasswell's title suggests the complex apparatus of governmental decision-making. The term "where" might be added to suggest the spatial or locational aspects of political decision.

Economists speak of "economizing," but unfortunately there is no similar word to designate the processes of political decision-making. Economists properly and frequently use the phrase *ceteris paribus*—other things being equal—as a means for holding constant or ignoring many non-economic variables, so that they may concentrate on problems of efficiency, welfare, income, price, supply, demand, and so forth. The area of interest of political science is precisely with these *other things*, even though techniques for handling them are still very primitive.

Decisions, whether in the public or in the private sphere, by definition require choices. As a matter of logic, to choose "A" means generally that one cannot also choose "non-A," although one may be able to choose a part of "A" and a part of "non-A." Choices imply the existence of one or more alternatives.

Many factors and forces determine alternatives available and influence the choices made. Political decisions are not made in a vacuum; they are not ends in themselves but a means by which societal goals are defined and implemented. Political decisions are responses to felt needs, and the identification and articulation of both needs and alternatives are what the political process is all about. Often, to be sure, the stimulus to action is vague and uncertain, and alternative courses of action are poorly defined. Cause and effect may not be tightly connected, and consequences may be inadequately understood or entirely disregarded. More often than not the full range of possible choices is not clearly spelled out or even determinable, which (among other things) has led Herbert Simon to suggest that the concept of maximization is not applicable to organizational decisions. He has developed instead the concept of "statisficing" to indicate that decisional choices require selection from among an often very limited range of possibilities.[3]

What choice will be made in a given situation is the result of many variables—chance, values, goals, facts, ideas, ideology, myths, reason, technology, personality, alliances, loyalties—all of which may interact to influence the choice, to shape the content of decision, to determine the parameters of actions, to set the time when a decision will or must be made.

Within this context of choice from among plural alternatives it is apparent that in the public sphere the processes of choosing may mean conflict, if for no other reason than that the choice of one alternative as against another will have differing consequences, working to the advantage of some and the disadvantage of others. It is this interaction, this struggle, that is the heart of politics and the political process. In Lasswell's phrase: Who gets what, when, how?

The nature and intensity of the struggle is itself a function of many variables. These variables are:

1. What is thought to be at stake, as perceived by those involved (and not all who have an interest are necessarily involved).
2. The judgment as to whether particular decisions are subject to change (and this may be based on an assessment of political power and influence).
3. The context or situation (including factors of timing) in which the need for decision arises.
4. The way in which the issue is drawn and by whom.
5. The extent to which decisions may be deliberately faced or simply left to the accretion of many small actions.

The place in the political system where decisions are made will also vary considerably, depending partly on the nature of the decision and partly on the structure of the system.

High school civics books and popular mythology imply that policy decisions reflect the positions of political parties operating through legislative bodies, with the Chief Executive having some role to play. In fact, American political parties are not issue or program oriented, one of the results of this being that a very large burden of policy decision-making is placed on the bureaus and agencies of government, often making them active participants in the political struggle and highly vulnerable to attack.

Decision-makers in the political process are people, acting as individuals or as groups, in organizations or in agencies, deliberately or casually, openly or secretly. This may be an obvious statement, but in this case, too, traditional democratic theory, moving from egalitarian premises, has tended to assume that each individual was identical with every other one, having uniform values, goals, aspirations, and behavior patterns.[4] At the same time, stress on a "government of laws, not of men" depersonalized the governmental process almost to the point where it became indecent to look at the people who operate the government apparatus.

In any case, it is clear that the psychological premises which supported these earlier attitudes are no longer tenable.

A distinguishing aspect of governmental decision-making, of course, is the fact that the decisions produced by the political process are supported by authority—the sanctions and power of government. Unquestionably, this fact intensifies the struggle for access to critical points of decision and makes issues of influence and power of major significance.[5]

American political decision-making is pragmatic rather than ideologically oriented. It is concerned with solving immediate problems rather than seeking to implement a systematic structure of values.[6] Few political decisions arise out of well-thought-out plans. They are, typically, immediate responses to particular problems, reflecting compromise and accommodation as well as conflict and struggle. Criteria for detached assessment of consequences are often not available and there is little interest in logical analysis of effects.

It is typical of the pragmatic in the political process that the initial impetus to TVA should have been a wartime shortage of nitrates,[7] even as the expansion of TVA thermal generating capacity was a response to the needs of another war and the secret exploitation of atomic energy at Oak Ridge.

Because of this problem-solving emphasis, the pattern of decisions in American government is not symmetrical nor neat. On the contrary, confusion and contradiction are frequent. That political decisions necessarily deal with undefined objectives in an uncertain future is a difficulty often compounded by the intangible and unmeasurable character of the values, motives, ideas, and ideologies which stimulate action. That controversy and debate result is thus normal, the purpose being to influence critical points of decision. And in the search for influence, the structuring of alliances and alignments, the building of power blocs of sufficient strength to gain at least short-run objectives is of major significance.

As important as the idea of struggle, conflict, and competition is the idea of accommodation—the readiness of those seeking favorable decisions not to press for tight, logically consistent decisions and to tolerate diverse ends and inconsistent objectives. The plural character of participant values and the general fluidity of our society tend to encourage easy accommodation and compromise and a constant shifting and adjusting of alliances and alignments. Something for everyone is easier to handle than tightly rationalized efficiency goals.

Many of us are uncomfortable with this description of political decision-making, still hoping for something like the eighteenth-century picture of rational behavior. But modern psychology strongly suggests that rationality in this simplistic sense was never attainable. The acknowledgment that political decisions with respect to values, with respect to goals, with respect to means, must often be based upon guess and judgment comes especially hard to the technician or specialist, be he engineer or economist, just because the methods of his discipline require focusing on a limited number of variables and the exclusion of others. And yet it is in this regard that the process of political decision-making takes on a kind of higher rationality, or at least necessity, in that it provides a means for making decisions before all the data has been gathered, before cause and effect relationships have been validated. The implicit overriding goal thus is the maintenance of a viable system and the avoidance of stalemate. This does not mean that the rational, the logical components in political decisions should not, where and as possible, be increased; it simply means that at any one time the extent to which rational calculation and logical analysis can provide full and adequate answers for societal decisions is very limited.

Political Forces in the Background and Founding of TVA

The decision to build the nitrate plants at Muscle Shoals and to construct Wilson Dam to provide electric power was an immediate response to the need for munitions in World War I. It did not emerge from careful planning nor from deliberate policy with respect to hydro power development by the government. Like defense-plant location decisions today, there were constant pressures under the 1916 Defense Act to spread the benefits of federal expenditures to various sections of the nation, and where possible to win votes and reward the faithful. Regard for economic principles of plant location received secondary consideration, if considered at all. The question of whether such rational values should have been considered is largely irrelevant.

At the same time, the record is clear that Muscle Shoals did represent one of the more attractive undeveloped water power sites in the nation, although there was some uncertainty as to whether the dam could be built quickly enough to provide munitions for a war already in its third year. But this risk was minimized by building steam plants to provide some power sooner.

It was important that the project be located in the solid Democratic South, for after all the Democrats were in power. And it was something less than chance that the senator from South Carolina, (Cotton) Ed Smith, was one of the principal advocates of including peacetime production of agricultural nitrates in the Muscle Shoals program, for the cotton South was at this time the principal user of agricultural nitrates.

The factors that influenced Congress in making decisions with respect to water development were described by the distinguished Harvard historian, A. B. Hart, in a paper delivered in 1887 before a joint meeting of the American Historical Association and the American Economic Association. Dr. Hart's paper, entitled "The Biography of a River and Harbor Bill,"[8] is a realistic description of the values operative in political decision-making in this field of policy. Professor Hart stated:

> the River and Harbor Committee never suffers for want of information in favor of appropriations. Unfortunately, though every job is likely to have an untiring advocate, the public interest has only such hard-worked and preoccupied members as look outside their own districts; there are a dozen pleas for expenditure, against one protest at extravagances . . . almost every Congressman is an interested party in some clause of the

> bill. . . . There is no such proof of the national importance of a bill as an item within it for one's own district. . . . The problem before the committee is always: How much may we put in without offending the newspapers? How much may we leave out without losing votes?

After indicating that almost half of the money appropriated would have only very local benefits, Professor Hart stated, "our bill, like most of its predecessors, contained provisions for the expenditure of money which could benefit only the owner of the waterfront, or the contractor, or the laborer."

Some sixty-four years later another Harvard professor, Arthur Maass, would publish *Muddy Waters: The Army Engineers and the Nation's Rivers*,[9] telling much the same story in a later edition. And it was undoubtedly in the tradition described by Professor Hart that the nitrate plants and Wilson Dam were begun.

But the real impetus to the TVA program came less from the decisions of 1916 and 1917 than from the discussions, debates, and controversies from 1918 to 1933 over what to do with the Muscle Shoals facilities. And it is at this point where the political process with respect to the ultimate decision to create TVA takes on a character of reasonableness, if not rationality, that distinguishes it from decisions to develop most other river basins.

In a sense, the decision processes that led to the creation of TVA in 1933 provide a classic example of how a democracy *should* work. It has been said that the amount of attention devoted to the Muscle Shoals problem from 1916 to 1933 was more extensive than on any other question considered by the Congress up to that time. Certainly here was no hidden maneuver, no plot to subvert the institutions of the United States. Rather, here was policy development involving the full panoply of political institutions, the deliberate interaction of ideas and people, the unhurried examination of many alternate proposals and propositions. Rarely in American history has one legislative problem received such extended and thorough consideration over so long a period of time. After World War II, in contrast, billions of dollars in war assets were disposed of with hardly any discussion at all.

Participants in the discussions and debates over Muscle Shoals held a variety of interests. There were, of course, the traditional interests in navigation development. In an era before cost-benefit studies, these interests were not much concerned with the efficiency of water navigation, any more than those who sought flood benefits worried about economic ratios. They only knew that Muscle Shoals was virtually impassable to their boats and barges, and they sought river improvement.

Flood control was not of major significance in the early discussions of the Muscle Shoals problem, but as flood damage increased, as the country became aware of and willing to have the federal government tackle flood problems (especially after the great Mississippi flood of 1927), and as arguments for control by means of storage reservoirs and river system design made more headway, more interest in flood control on the Tennessee also developed. Changes in technology as well as changing concepts with respect to the role of government were a part of the context of political choice.

During the twenties, farm interests looked to Muscle Shoals for agricultural nitrogen. At the time, this meant primarily Southern cotton and tobacco interests, for the general use of synthetic fertilizers was still many years in the future. Hence, some American farm leaders turned to the Shoals for cheaper nitrogen; some farm circles hoped in part that the well-known offer by Henry Ford to purchase the Shoals would be accepted and that Ford would mass-produce fertilizers at a low price.

It is noteworthy, however, that through the years of debate Senator Norris remained skeptical of the feasibility of government nitrate production, although in most of his legislative proposals he included provisions for this function. His major interest was electric power development, although for this interest there were few ardent supporters.

A kind of negative impetus to the TVA program lay in the concern of some congressmen that the government should receive a fair return for its original more than $100 million investment in Muscle Shoals. Such concern was voiced, for example, by Congressman James of Michigan in a forceful minority report in 1926.

The result was that although the majority of Congress probably favored the general ideas of private development of the Shoals properties—after all, most of the debate as what to do with Muscle Shoals occurred at the height of the Coolidge and Hoover boom—the terms of private offers were always so inadequate as to permit a small group of legislators to rally sufficient votes to defeat them.

But the major issue in the Muscle Shoals controversy was not navigation or flood control or fertilizers or a fair return to the government for its chemical plant investments. The major issue was hydro power development. Initially it was control of Wilson Dam power, and ultimately it was control of the entire Tennessee system. This has remained a primary source of political conflict with respect to TVA.

The power fight was not peculiar to the Tennessee River, although many of the battles have occurred here. From the time that hydro generation of electricity became feasible in the late nineteenth century, promoters in the American tradition of exploitation had sought and received rights to develop the more attractive water power sites on the nation's rivers. These awards usually took the form of special legislation enacted by Congress, in many cases granting perpetual rights. In 1903 President Theodore Roosevelt vetoed an attempt to grant to one N. F. Thompson and associates the authority to construct a dam and power station at Muscle Shoals.[10] After that, almost day by day, the controversy over control of power development grew more and more intense. A part of the issue was settled by the creation of the Federal Power Commission in 1920,[11] but this represented only the beginning of the struggle to control the development of the Tennessee and specifically to benefit from wartime public expenditures on Wilson Dam.

While the details of this struggle cannot be covered here, the constancy of Senator Norris to the principle that the *public* should benefit from *public* expenditures must be noted. Year in and year out, although not from a Tennessee Valley state, he pressed for authorization of public operation of the hydro facilities for public benefit. And it is worth emphasizing that his persistence, plus the inadequacy of alternate proposals, led in 1928 to the passage of a bill that was only slightly different from the TVA Act of 1933—this at the height of the Coolidge free enterprise boom. But President Coolidge vetoed the bill as did Hoover a similar one in 1931.[12]

The interest of Franklin Delano Roosevelt in conservation led naturally to his supporting the Norris proposal for the development of the Tennessee. And to the Norris program FDR contributed a broader concept of resource development, although no one in the early 1930's really had a very clear idea of what development meant or how it was to be achieved. This broader concept, inadequately imbedded in sections 22 and 23 of the TVA Act which stress studies and investigations, was never clearly formulated as a statutory goal. Undoubtedly, concern for economic development was a factor in the selection of the original members of the TVA Board of Directors, although these distinguished men qualified for many other reasons, including their acceptability to a variety of interest groups. In any case, TVA was left largely to itself in giving meaning and content to concepts of regional and economic development.

Three points should be stressed in this connection. The first is that in the depth of the depression the goal of economic development (often stated at that time in terms of economic planning) was widely, though often vaguely and uncritically, accepted as a proper role of government. As a result, not much attention was paid by supporters of TVA to the sufficiency of the TVA Act in this regard, and it never proved tactically possible later to improve the statutory basis for regional development activities.

Second, the concepts and techniques for economic development in 1933 were not adequately understood, either by political leaders or by economists. The desire to improve the region's economy (as well as the nation's) was great, but the variety of means that might be employed for reaching that goal were less well perceived than they seem to be today. In any case, political decisions are, unfortunately, always limited by the status of knowledge at a particular time.

Third, it was typical of American political decision-making to leave the formulation of the agency mission to the agency itself.

This, inevitably, assures that programs (and the agencies sponsoring them) over which there is great diversity of opinion are likely to be deeply involved in the political struggle.

Political History of TVA since 1933

The political history of TVA since 1933 can perhaps be divided into three distinct periods, each of which deserves at least brief characterization: the New Deal period, 1933 to approximately 1940; the World War II period, 1940 to 1946; and the postwar period, 1946 to the inauguration of the late President Kennedy. The last few years of the immediate present probably mark the beginning of a fourth period, but it is too soon to comment on these more recent developments.

The New Deal period of TVA, like that of many agencies, was marked by an atmosphere of social daring and experimentation. The problems of economic recovery were acute and proposed solutions were meant to be bold, even though in retrospect they may sometimes seem naïve or ill-conceived.

Many of the forces which were involved in the fifteen years of TVA pre-history continued to be important after TVA had become a reality. Wide national interest in the project broadened the support base, but it also increased opposition. In retrospect, the critical political problems of these initial years appeared to be:

1. The constitutional litigation on which the very life of TVA depended.[13]
2. The conflicts among members of the Board of Directors.[14]
3. The congressional investigation of TVA.[15]
4. The ferment of activity and ideas associated with the formulation of a program and the development of an agency philosophy.[16]

Each of these four points might be developed in great detail, but I will only comment on one feature that pervades all four and that is typical of the American political process. Although, as pointed out, there was a great quantity of debate and discussion preceding the enactment of the TVA statute, it was left to pragmatic day-to-day decisions by administrators and agency heads to give form and substance to the TVA program. To be sure, that program had to be consistent with the statute—and lawyers played a major role in shaping the final product—yet there was no clear idea of what TVA was to do and even less as to how it was to proceed. Basic policy questions of engineering design of river-control works were left to the agency to determine. Even greater uncertainty prevailed with respect to power policy and fertilizer development. And as for concepts of regional development, these were perceived in the vaguest terms.

This is no criticism of TVA but rather reflects the extent to which the political system places responsibility for these types of decisions on agencies in the executive branch, not necessarily at the presidential level, but often quite far down the line. And it is just because these responsibilities rest with the administrative agency that such agencies often find themselves embroiled in political conflict and controversy, as a variety of interests scramble for access to points of decision.

Personality factors aside, it is clear that the conflict among members of the Board of Directors reflected differing views as to mission and approach. Here were major choice problems and it is not surprising that the process of choosing led to conflict and struggle. It was true then, and it is still true now, that a regional agency had no appropriate political forum to which to turn for resolution of policy differences. There was no regional legislature, no technique for regional authorizing referenda. The issues had to be dealt with internally, and yet they had to meet with acceptance. Experience indicates that the national Congress is not prone to spend much time with regional matters, although certainly the 1939 investigation of TVA took a great deal of the time of a few congressmen. But the investigation itself produced few policy results. It, like the litigation, served rather as a kind of refining fire for the agency; it provided the occasion and a kind of forum for a searching examination of objectives, authority, and operating methods, the net result probably having been a narrowing of original goals. But these experiences reflected typical pragmatic responses to particular problems rather than rational planning in the formulation of a guiding philosophy for the agency. In this vein, results are rationalizations of what is and what is judged to be possible rather than products of deliberate and careful formulation of goals, plans, and programs.

It is no wonder that some foreign visitors, imbued with ideas of economic planning, have left the Tennessee Valley baffled and confused. They have failed to perceive the nature of the American political process and to understand that what they saw in the Tennessee Valley was not untypical of political decision-making generally.

Before leaving this early period of TVA history, something must be said about the relationships of the agency to people of the Valley. Initially, and particularly when they observed the ferment and confusion within the agency in these early years, there was apparently much skepticism. But by the end of this period, the support of large numbers of Valley citizens became a force of considerable importance to the continuance of TVA, reflected among other things in the behavior of most Valley congressmen and senators. Motives behind this support, of course, varied greatly. But in many cases it rested on more than simply being appreciative of the benefits bestowed by federal expenditures. Certainly it was more intense and I think more understanding than that found in most river basins where too often the pork barrel has been substituted for the cracker barrel as the symbol of local democracy. In the case of this Valley, it seems to me, there was a widespread and deeply rooted sense of participation in a significant program.

Philip Selznick, in an oft-cited book, *TVA and the Grass Roots*,[17] has advanced the thesis that TVA as an organization was, in fact, "coopted" by the influentials in the Valley. In my opinion, Selznick, too, misunderstands the nature of the political process and of the relationships between citizens and government agencies serving them. He argued that government agencies take on the values of the leaders in the area in which they operate. More broadly, he suggested that government agencies must make strategic and tactical judgments in order to gain support for their continuation. Insofar as Selznick is merely suggesting that government agencies are also involved in the political process, his position is a truism. But Selznick overlooks the extent to which relationships and influence are reciprocal. People influence agency personnel and agency personnel influence people in a complex web of interaction, conditioned by many forces and factors, among which program acceptability is always tactically important. The fact of interaction is obvious; the suggestion that a price is exacted for support oversimplifies problems of values by ignoring the plural forces at work and overlooking the impact of ideas, motives, and persuasion on political behavior.

The war period in TVA's political life may be touched on very briefly. For TVA, it was a period of consolidation during which many of the previous controversies seemed forgotten or muted. Overwhelming praise characterized TVA's tenth anniversary. Even the Chicago *Tribune* carried a grudging tribute.

Perhaps the war encouraged a moratorium on certain kinds of political controversy. In any case, the demand for electric energy and for munitions meant a sizable stepping up of the power and chemical programs, so that by the end of the war most of the river structures were completed, with thermal power becoming an increasingly important factor in the supply picture, and chemical facilities were greatly expanded.

Note that I said the controversies were muted, that there seemed to be a moratorium on certain kinds of political controversies. In many cases, the forum for conflict during the war shifted to the executive branch and war agencies. A busy President could not be bothered with TVA's problems, so the struggle went on in the Bureau of the Budget and in agencies like the War Production Board. In a sense, the conflicts at these points of decision only foreshadowed the postwar situation.

With the Eightieth Congress—the body labeled the "do-nothing Congress" by President Truman—TVA's political troubles revived, only to be intensified during the Eisenhower administration when the President himself expressed concern over what he considered the "creeping socialism" of TVA.

By this time the political environment within which TVA was operating was much different from that in the initial period of growth in the mid-thirties. Prosperity had taken the place of depression; strong antigovernmental biases were more frequently expressed; and interest in broadly conceived regional development lagged. In the popular mind, development became a problem associated with conquered countries or emerging nations; it was not something to worry about in the United States. Domestic resource programs were curtailed, although water development activity continued.

In TVA, for a variety of reasons, development took on a narrower focus, emphasizing particularly the problems of electric power. It would be interesting to examine in chronological order the political struggles in which TVA was involved after 1946, particularly during the Eisenhower years, and to attempt to measure their intensity. But this must remain for a future article. I want instead to examine some of the ideas and concepts which have been particularly associated with TVA and which have had a considerable effect upon political decisions with respect to water development.

Key Lessons from TVA's Experience

As asserted earlier American political decisions are seldom based on ideology or ideas but rather are simply pragmatic responses to particular problems. Often values, beliefs, concepts, and ideas that are associated with particular programs are *ex post facto* rationalizations or simply the product of publicists and propagandists. To some, this may sound cynical and offensive because it seems so contrary to standards of rationality. The place of reason in society would itself be a topic for extended discussion.[18] It is introduced here simply to emphasize the fact that in many ways TVA has been responsible for or associated with a number of ideas and concepts that have had a significant impact upon water development decisions both in the Valley and more generally. In this respect, in my opinion, TVA differs considerably from most federal agencies in that an explicit body of doctrine—ideology if you will—has developed around its program.

In this final part of my discussion, then, I want to identify several of these key ideas that have been associated with the TVA program over the years, ideas which have in a variety of ways been important elements of political decisions affecting TVA and water development generally. Three ideas are especially important: (1) The idea of comprehensive regional development including the integration of land and water programs; (2) unified administration of regional development programs; and (3) TVA as a symbol of "socialism."

Regional Development. TVA remains a symbol of regional development, although as already suggested the meaning of the concept has never been precise and many problems associated with development have never been resolved. As indicated, TVA's authority in this regard was, from many points of view, less than adequate. In its first few years this seemed to be only a minor impediment, for collaboration with other New Deal programs often resulted in impressive results. REA (Rural Electrification Administration) was one such result, stimulated initially by TVA. Another was the program of appliance financing, now long forgotten, which sought to encourage the purchase of appliances and thus to expand the consumption of electricity. Moreover, the record is clear that in its early days TVA used its meager authority in such ways as to stimulate broader development action whenever possible. The list of these "byproduct" results is long and impressive and includes such diverse activities as encouraging public administration education, stimulating bookmobiles and rural libraries, strengthening rural health services, and initiating studies which drastically changed the railroad freight rate structure.

But the fundamental question of TVA's developmental role has never been resolved, largely because it was politically not possible to have the issue resolved. Even the narrower question of the role of electric energy in regional development has never been answered fully, as is suggested by the difficulties of reconciling watershed and power-service area boundaries. That electric power at low rates is an economic boon can readily be conceded; that it is an effective vehicle for achieving regional economic growth and development still remains to be proved. On this question Professor Gilbert White has stated:

> In both the Hoover Dam and TVA examples, regional effects were intimated but not planned, then enjoyed but not managed. They were

> dimly perceived at the start, hailed when apparent, and the subject of earnest study after the decisions as to major river regulation works had been made. [Such gauges of economic well-being as per capita income, diversification of industry and agriculture, and stability of employment] . . . entered the discussion of the wisdom of the projects more as rationalizations than as prior justifications.[19]

As for the intimate relationship between land programs and water programs, the record is more one of faith than of action. The conception of this relationship has always been popular, but bureaucratic conflicts with national land-use agencies defeated all but the most minimal attempts to accomplish anything on this score. While the TVA agricultural program, especially in its massive stages, brought many benefits to farmers of the region and no doubt contributed to agricultural improvement, such results rested primarily on nationally oriented fertilizer provisions of the statute and were with difficulty fitted into a regional development mold.

At present, the virtual preemption of watershed programs by the U. S. Department of Agriculture tends to negate the idea of a planned interrelationship between land and channel programs, although the fact of a physical connection between what occurs on the land and in the stream is obvious, even when not planned.

Unified Administration. The concept of unified regional administration has often been stressed as one of the unique ideas developed by TVA.[20] It might be noted, however, that as the scope of the TVA program narrowed, the significance of unified administration diminished. Yet, the idea of unified administration has been regarded as one of TVA's great contributions, imitated, at least superficially, at many places in the world.

I would argue, moreover, that immediately after the war the threat of creating regional agencies like TVA in other basins did more to bring about a semblance of coordination of federal basin activities than any other single thing. But meanwhile unified administration of regional development in the Tennessee Valley was resisted, and when TVA sought to relate other federal programs to regional needs, it was often portrayed as uncooperative and petulant.

TVA and Socialism. This is the great issue in which TVA has been and continues to be embroiled. It is an intriguing issue because its terms have been set not by TVA nor by its supporters, but by its opponents. And there are few examples in American governmental history of such vehement and persistent hostility to a government program. Perhaps the great debates in the early days of the republic over internal improvements or over the National Bank are analogous.

To many persons, the issue of TVA (even after thirty years) is an ideological one—Mr. Eisenhower's "creeping socialism." But as I have already indicated, the TVA program evolved out of typically pragmatic circumstances. It has had few deep ideological roots. Most of the ideas associated with TVA have been *ex post facto* rationalizations of necessarily immediate decisions.

Rarely has the question of supplying water to urban residents been considered as a matter of socialism, yet most of our urban water supply comes from government-owned and operated systems. In Nebraska all electric power is supplied by public agencies, and some public power is found in many parts of the nation. There is, in fact, little objection to public power generation and transmission from the now very extensive system of river-control works constructed under Army or reclamation auspices. Although these various situations have at times involved controversy, that controversy has rarely been couched in ideological terms—these government programs have rarely been labeled "socialistic."

How can this be? Why has TVA been singled out by its opponents as the symbol of socialism? The simple answer, it seems to me, is that TVA has been unusually successful in accomplishing its power objectives and its very success is regarded as a continuing threat to the utility industry of the nation, both because TVA shows that government need not be inefficient and bumbling and because of particular TVA policies.

The private power industry is no carriage industry fighting the automobile! This is one of the major industrial sectors of our economy which because of its monopolistic position in particular markets and its constitutionally guaranteed profits represents millions in invested capital and millions in expected income. This is substantial economic power. Insurance companies, trust funds, retirement funds—all rely on the steady dividend and interest returns from electric power stocks and bonds.

But is TVA really a threat to the utility industry? No responsible official (to my knowledge) has ever suggested the nationalization of the power industry in this country. At the same time it must be recognized, however, that a threat may exist in the minds of those threatened, based on inferences arising from the actions of those regarded as threatening.

The yardstick about which we used to hear a great deal was never regarded as a threat. But the fact that TVA (with Federal Power Commission help) established the distinction in power accounting between generating costs, transmission costs, and distribution costs is a threat because it has bared the fact of high profits at the distribution end. No businessman likes his customers to know on which part of his operation he makes his profits.

The other major issue that leads private utilities to fear the TVA example is, it seems to me, the fact that TVA is the sole supplier of electric energy in its service area. The charges of socialism have not been raised with respect to power development in other river basins for three reasons. First, in no other river basin is power generated by the federal government the sole source of supply. Second, in no other region has the federal power agency assumed responsibility for meeting all power demands of its service area. And third, in no other region is there such a convenient and visible target for opposition attacks. With visibility goes vulnerability and, as suggested in this case, the terms of the conflict are not defined by TVA but by those who oppose it.

Conclusions

In summary, then, TVA exemplifies many aspects of the political process as related to water development, although in many instances the TVA experience has involved extremes. Partly at its own initiative and partly at the initiative of those opposed to it, TVA has brought up for discussion a range of significant ideas and concepts which have had marked impact on the public approach to water development generally.

For reasons associated particularly with power policy, TVA and the development of the Tennessee River have constantly been involved in political struggles and controversies. These controversies, rather than being causes for alarm or regret, have served a useful purpose in bringing issues for decision to the fore. So long as our political system operates as it does, this will be the way in which decisions are best made.

What of the future? Many of the issues associated with TVA have been settled. In the process, not only the setting for decisions but the deciders have changed. It would be unrealistic to suggest that TVA today is no different from the TVA of ten or twenty or thirty years ago. The decisions that TVA leaders have faced, decisions of substance and decisions of tactics, have not been easy ones. The process itself has had its effects and in political decision-making martyrdom has few rewards. I doubt that the future will be without its difficulties, although I suspect that the next thirty years will be less controversial just because the program has changed. But one major issue will continue to be raised and that, of course, is the issue of power policy. Here TVA's success guarantees continual opposition, given the biases and fears of the business community. And so long as politics is concerned with "Who gets what, when, how?" the possibility of conflict and struggle remains—and this is the primary characteristic of political decision-making.

References

1. Harold D. Lasswell, *Politics: Who Gets What, When, How* (New York: McGraw-Hill, 1936).
2. The most significant work on the political process is still perhaps David B. Truman, *The Governmental Process* (New York: Alfred A. Knopf, 1955).
3. Herbert A. Simon, "Theories of Decision-Making in Economics and Behavioral Science," in *The American Economic Review,* XLIX (June, 1959), 262.

4. In addition to Truman, *op. cit.,* who emphasizes group concepts, see also Bertram Gross, *The Legislative Struggle* (New York: McGraw-Hill, 1953); and Charles B. Hagan, "The Group in Political Science," in *Approaches to the Study of Politics* (Evanston: Northwestern University Press, 1958), pp. 38–51.
5. See Norman Wengert, *Natural Resources and the Political Struggle* (New York: Doubleday and Co., 1955).
6. See Norman Wengert, "The Ideological Basis of Conservation and Natural Resources Policies and Programs," in *The Annals of the American Academy of Political and Social Science*, CCCXLIV (Nov., 1962), 65–75.
7. This summary of TVA legislative history is based on Norman Wengert, "Antecedents of TVA: The Legislative History of Muscle Shoals," in *Agricultural History*, XXVI (Oct., 1952), 141–147.
8. Albert B. Hart, in *Practical Essays on American Government* (New York: Longmans, Green, and Co., 1894), pp. 206–232; this is a reprint of the 1887 paper.
9. Cambridge, Mass.: Harvard University Press, 1951.
10. U. S., *Congressional Record*, 57th Cong., 2nd Sess., 1903, XXXVI, 3071–3073.
11. *Federal Power Act of 1920*, U.S., *Statutes at Large*, XLI, 1063.
12. Wengert, "Antecedents of TVA," *op. cit.,* p. 146.
13. The major TVA cases were *Ashwander* v. *T.V.A.*, 297 U.S. 288 (1936), and *Tennessee Electric Power Co.* v. *T.V.A.,* 306 U.S. 118 (1939).
14. See Herman Pritchett, *The Tennessee Valley Authority* (Chapel Hill: University of North Carolina Press, 1943), especially chap. vii.
15. U. S. Congress, Joint Committee on Investigation of TVA, *Hearings*, 75th Cong., 3rd Sess., 1939, and U. S. Congress, Senate, *Report*, 76th Cong., 1st Sess., Senate Doc. 56. For a general summary of the investigation, see D. L. Marlett, "TVA Investigation," in *Journal of Land and Public Utility Economics*, XV (May, 1939), 212–224, and *ibid.* (Aug., 1939), 360–364.
16. See Pritchett, *op. cit.*, and David E. Lilienthal, *TVA: Democracy on the March* (New York: Harper & Brothers, 1944).
17. Philip Selznick, *TVA and the Grass Roots* (Berkeley: University of California Press, 1949).
18. Paul Diesing, *Reason in Society: Five Types of Decisions and Their Social Conditions* (Urbana: University of Illinois Press, 1962).
19. Gilbert F. White, "A Perspective of River Basin Development," *Law and Contemporary Problems*, XXII (Spring, 1957), 157–186.
20. David E. Lilienthal, *op. cit.*, gave special emphasis to this concept.

Identical Pricing and TVA: Toward More Effective Competition

RONALD H. WOLF is the holder of B.B.A. and M.A. degrees from the University of Washington and the Ph.D. degree from Vanderbilt University. He has been with the University of Tennessee Department of Economics since 1958 and now holds the title of Associate Professor.

The Tennessee Valley Authority is the nation's largest single producer of electric power, generating about 10 per cent of the power produced in the country.[1] As a large enterprise its purchases of manufactured products, raw materials, and services are substantial, ranging in recent years anywhere from slightly over $120 million to more than $500 million each year.[2]

In carrying out its statutory obligation to do its "purchasing in accordance with or in a manner that will provide free competition," the Authority's Board of Directors has established that formal advertising rather than negotiation will be the principal procedure used in procurement.[3] Thus, in contrast to many federal agencies, TVA makes most of its purchases through the bid procedure, which in recent years has accounted for about 95 per cent of the total value of contract awards—a record of devotion to the use of sealed bids unmatched by any other federal agency.[4]

Ever since its beginning in 1933, the Tennessee Valley Authority has been getting, from time to time, identical bid prices on some products in response to its invitations to bid. Although identical prices may result from competition, they may also result either from concerted action on the part of rivals to act as one on price, or from discrimination in absorbing freight in the case of some customers in order to achieve equality.[5] Since identical prices may be the result of either concerted action or discrimination, they are always suspect until the explanation of the identity has been made clear.

When construction of dams was a major activity, interest centered on cement where the industry's use of a multiple basing-point system resulted in identical prices at various delivery points, irrespective of the location of the cement mill. Dr. Arthur E. Morgan, first TVA board chairman, brought the matter to the attention of the White House and even threatened that TVA would set up its own cement manufacturing plant. President Franklin D. Roosevelt and Secretary of the Interior Harold L. Ickes favored getting the cement industry to quote f.o.b mill prices, rather than delivered prices, on government contracts. However, the industry refused and the matter was dropped at the time. Later, Morgan's views and testimony were part of the successful assault on the cement industry's pricing practices. The matter was climaxed in 1948 with the Supreme Court's affirmation of the Federal Trade Commission's finding of concerted action—an unfair method of competition under Section 5 of the Federal Trade Commission Act—and of price discrimination damaging to competition—a practice illegal under the Robinson-Patman Act.[6]

Under the Federal Property and Administrative Services Act of 1949, the Tennessee Valley Authority and other civilian agencies covered by the act were required "to report to the Attorney General identical bids received after advertising when, in the opinion of the head of the agency, they evidenced violations of the antitrust laws."[7] TVA also supplied information on identical bids to the Select Committee on Small Business of the House of Representatives at the latter's request. Such reporting to these two bodies continued for a period of not more than one year until both requested that the reporting be stopped.[8]

Apparently the Attorney General was flooded with reports of identical bidding, especially from the military agencies which followed reporting procedures similar to those followed by the civilian agencies. In making reports, "the military agencies adopted the view that they were obligated to refer to the Attorney General all identical bids whether or not they evidenced a violation of the antitrust laws. They took this view ostensibly because military buyers could not be expected to detect antitrust violations and the only criterion for selection of cases for referral to the Attorney General was the presence of identical bids."[9] The Department of Justice in 1952 secured the cooperation of reporting agencies in limiting reports to those cases where the purchasing officer thought that illegal antitrust practices might be present. Under this revised procedure reports dropped drastically, from a total of 7,554 reports for the two calendar years of 1950 and 1951, to a total of 60 for the two calendar years of 1953 and 1954.[10]

Observing that the pendulum had apparently swung too far in reducing the number of reports filed, the Antitrust Division of the

Department of Justice in 1957 initiated negotiations with civilian and military agencies seeking to improve reporting procedures and to expand the volume of reports containing evidence of antitrust law violations. On March 17, 1959, the General Services Administration issued its Federal Procurement Regulations, which set out revised procedures for civilian agencies in reporting possible antitrust violations. Emphasis was still placed not on the reporting of identical prices but on the reporting of suspect prices which appeared to violate the antitrust laws. However, greater attention was paid to indicating the character of the information essential to the making of decisions as to when identical prices indicate a violation of the antitrust laws.[11]

Unearthing the Electrical Products Conspiracies

On May 13, 1959, the Tennessee Valley Authority announced that its Board of Directors had recently authorized the purchasing department to make identical bids public and that under that authority it was disclosing three instances of identical price quotations involving conductor cable, transformers, and weed killer. Hitherto, the agency had announced only the low, successful bidder in its contract awards; henceforth, said the agency, it would disclose all identical bids submitted by manufacturers on the agency's purchases of equipment and materials. TVA, in explaining this change in policy, noted that for years some United States manufacturers, primarily in the electrical field, had quoted the same prices regularly. An agency spokesman said that the board took the action "because the occurrence of identical bids reflected a situation that we thought was of public interest and possibly of public concern."[12]

The announcement of this change in policy set off a chain of events that led ultimately to the uncovering of a number of conspiracies involving price-fixing and bid-rigging in various electrical product lines. Curious to find out more about identical bidding, a staff writer for the Knoxville *News-Sentinel,* Julian Granger, made arrangements to visit Paul Fahey, head of TVA procurement, in

Chattanooga.[13] Armed with facts which Fahey put at his disposal, Granger published a series of three supplementary articles to the original news story released on May 13, the first of which appeared in the *News-Sentinel* on May 17, 1959.[14] In his article of May 17, Granger disclosed that a sampling of TVA's purchasing records back to October, 1956, revealed twenty-four instances of matched bids, with at least forty-seven large and small United States manufacturers taking part in identical bidding on a wide variety of products.

Milton Britten, Washington correspondent of the Knoxville *News-Sentinel*, called Granger's articles to the attention of Senator Estes Kefauver, chairman of the Senate Subcommittee on Antitrust and Monopoly.[15] Kefauver alerted the Department of Justice,[16] wrote to TVA for additional information,[17] sent Paul Rand Dixon, counsel and staff director of the subcommittee, to visit TVA's purchasing director,[18] and announced that his subcommittee would conduct an investigation and hold hearings on the matter.[19]

Alerted, the Department of Justice also took action. It sent William L. Maher, chief of the Middle Atlantic office of its Antitrust Division, to visit TVA's procurement chief and obtain more information.[20] On June 30, 1959, the Department of Justice—armed with information that it had been gathering since 1957, plus new information furnished it by TVA—confirmed that it had authorized a federal grand jury at Philadelphia to look into identical bids in the electrical equipment industry.[21]

On July 21, 1959, the Knoxville *News-Sentinel* reported that the Tennessee Valley Authority, in its current weekly newsletter, had announced another instance of identical bidding. In this case the Authority had issued four separate invitations for bids; two called for bids on 3,000 insulators, one on 12,000 insulators, and one on 15,000 insulators, for a total of 33,000 insulators. Invitations were sent to eight companies of which seven responded, submitting identical bids on each of the four requests.

Eliminating those bidders who were not in labor surplus areas, TVA pared the number of firms to be considered to three. Because the plant of one of these was closed owing to a strike, the agency did not consider its bid but awarded the contracts as equally as possible to the two remaining suppliers, Lapp Insulator Company and General Electric Company. As the agency was quoted in the press: "Lapp was awarded the contract for 15,000 insulators at a cost of $51,000, and GE received the contracts for 3,000 and 12,000 insulators at a total cost of $51,000. The recipient of the remaining contract for 3,000 insulators at a cost of $10,200 was determined in a drawing, and Lapp was successful."

The press report went on to say that Lapp, General Electric, and the five other firms involved in the incident had emerged in the same role throughout the paper's study of earlier matching bids, dating back to October, 1956. Earlier in 1959 Lapp had been among the identical bidders in regard to insulators. The press study had also disclosed that Lapp had been among the identical bidders in five other TVA purchases of such equipment as bushings for transformers and power circuit breakers. As Clarence C. Walton and Frederick W. Cleveland, Jr., have pointed out: "As events progressed, this insulator contract proved to be the key to the whole series of cases which developed out of the investigation."[22]

The Senate Subcommittee on Antitrust and Monopoly held hearings on identical bidding in Knoxville on September 28, 29, and 30, 1959. At the hearings it was disclosed that, from April 1, 1956, to the time of the hearings, TVA had received identical bids on twenty-two different products. The products included aluminum cable steel reinforced conductor, carbon electrodes and connecting pins, carrier current equipment, condenser tubing, industrial salt, insulators, bus type insulators, station post type insulators, suspension insulators, lightning arresters, oil circuit breakers, portland cement, steel drums, transformer bushings, auxiliary transformers, current transformers, distribution transformers, 15-kilovolt current transformers, 161-kilovolt potential transformers, potential transformers, power transformers, and weed killer.[23] It was also hinted at the hearings that on some sealed-bid business there seemed to be a regular rotation of the winning bids among various suppliers.[24] This hint turned out to be significant because subsequent developments made clear that there was not only price-fixing but also bid-rigging in some electrical product lines. Moreover, the hearing records were put at the disposal of the Department of Justice in Philadelphia,[25] and TVA continued to supply the subcommittee and the Department of Justice with all new instances of identical bids, at their requests.[26]

In the meantime the grand jury investigation which had been launched was continuing. According to Vernon A. Mund: "The grand jury proceedings were about to close in the usual and routine way without evidence of conspiracy. Only at the last minute, it appears, did the conscience of one witness trouble him so much that he decided to tell the truth. This provided an opening for all of the cases."[27] Apparently it was a Lapp Insulator Company official who, when "asked the right questions," gave "the right answers."[28] With this break, the work of the grand jury multiplied greatly, eventually requiring not one jury but five.[29]

On February 16 and 17, 1960, the first seven of what finally turned out to be twenty indictments were returned. According to Walton and Cleveland: "Arraignment on the charges came in the middle of March 1960, before Judge J. Cullen Ganey, sitting in the United States District Court in the Eastern District of Pennsylvania. The two major companies, General Electric and Westinghouse, entered pleas of not guilty. The others asked to plead *nolo contendere*."[30] The government strongly opposed the *nolo* pleas, a view which Judge Ganey accepted. At the arraignment for pleadings in April, Allis-Chalmers Manufacturing Company entered pleas of guilty, and I-T-E Circuit Breaker Company entered pleas of guilty on two of seven indictments.[31] The others pleaded not guilty. "From this point on, Allis-Chalmers cooperated wholeheartedly with the government, making available," according to Walton and Cleveland, "documents and witnesses to show the nature of its involvement, not only in the cases to which it had pleaded, but in other conspiracies in which it was involved."[32]

Additional indictments were handed down in May, June, and

September, the final one being returned on October 20, 1960.[33] Altogether there were twenty indictments covering the sale of twenty different pieces of equipment used in the generation, transmission, and distribution of electric power. The products involved were bushings, circuit breakers, low-voltage circuit breakers, condensers, industrial control equipment, insulators, isolated phase bus, lightning arresters, low-voltage distribution equipment, open-fuse cutouts, power capacitors, power switching equipment, marine switchgear, power switchgear, distribution transformers, instrument transformers, network transformers, power transformers, turbine-generators, and watt-hour meters.[34]

Altogether twenty-nine companies and forty-five executives were indicted on federal charges of price-fixing, bid-rigging, and market-sharing. None of the cases went to trial, as all pleas were or were changed to either guilty or no contest.[35] On February 6 and 7, 1961, Judge Ganey set the sentences. Seven executives received thirty-day prison terms, and twenty-four others received suspended thirty-day terms and were put on probation for five years. Corporate and personal fines totaled approximately $1,900,000.

Aftermath of the Criminal Cases

The conclusion of the criminal cases did not end the episode. For one thing, buyers of the twenty products have availed themselves of their right to bring damage suits, a task made easier by the fact that the government sought and obtained pleas of guilty in the seven "most serious" indictments. These products included circuit breakers, condensers, industrial control equipment, power switchgear, power switching equipment, power transformers, and turbine-generators. The annual sales of these products amounted to about two-thirds of all the sales involved.[36]

Governmental action to recover damages for the non-competitive prices charged began on March 14, 1961, when the Department of Justice and the Tennessee Valley Authority, in joint action, filed a civil complaint in Philadelphia seeking to recover more than $12,000,000 in damages from five manufacturers of large outdoor oil and air circuit breakers.[37] Subsequently, the government filed ten additional suits, in five of which TVA joined as plaintiff with the United States.[38]

General Electric Company was the only defendant named in all eleven governmental suits, and it was with this company that the government first reached an out-of-court settlement. In July, 1962, General Electric agreed to pay $7,470,000 to the government, of which TVA's share was $6,470,000. This settlement involved total purchases of about $69,600,000, of which TVA accounted for about $57,600,000.[39]

In April, 1963, the government agreed to a $272,450 settlement involving seven companies which were defendants in three of the government's eleven damage suits. Of this sum, it was reported that $179,715 would go to the Tennessee Valley Authority.[40] In May, 1963, Westinghouse Electric Corporation agreed to pay $800,000 in settlement on purchases which had amounted to about $15,700,000. Of this sum, it was reported that TVA would receive $430,000.[41] As of August 31, 1965, TVA and other federal government agencies had secured $8,800,000 from twelve companies in settlement of civil damage suits.[42]

In spite of the handicaps and problems that accompany damage suits, by the early part of September, 1965, almost 2,000 suits had been filed against the defendant firms. Two-thirds of the cases had already been settled, almost all of them out of court. Most of the remaining 719 suits, it was said, were small. At that time, General Electric had paid about $236 million and Allis-Chalmers about $45 million in claims. Westinghouse, it was said, had set aside $110 million to cover its suits. Both General Electric and Westinghouse asserted that they had already settled about 99 per cent of the dollar value of the suits brought against them. Reports have not been available for the other defendants, but it has been estimated that total damages for all defendants will run to $400 or $500 million by the time the last suit is ended.[43]

The episode has continued, too, in regard to the companion civil actions which the government filed against the firms to restrain them permanently from any future anticompetitive activity. Further, the government asked that Judge Ganey direct every company to withdraw its present price lists for heavy electrical equipment within sixty days after he granted the injunction and issue a new price list "on the basis of its individual cost figures and individual judgment as to profits."[44]

Late in May, 1961, the C. H. Wheeler Manufacturing Company, producer of condensers, became the first defendant to accept a consent decree.[45] The firm agreed to review and redetermine, within the following year, all book prices and conditions of sale for its condenser products. The enterprise was also required to itemize the cost of condensers in any bids or quotations for electrical equipment which included condensers. It had to be prepared to swear that all bids for condenser sales were prepared secretly and without collusion with other manufacturers. Finally, the company agreed to refrain from selling at "unreasonably low prices" where there was a "reasonable probability" that the low prices would have an anticompetitive effect.[46]

When the Department of Justice asked several other defendants, including General Electric, to sign similar decrees, General Electric balked, objecting to the provision prohibiting it from selling at "unreasonably low prices" with anticompetitive *effect*. The company suggested a counterproposal: it would agree not to sell at "unreasonably low prices" with anticompetitive *intent*. The government rejected this offer, and the impasse continued for over a year until agreement was finally reached in September, 1962.[47] The government deleted the "fair pricing clause," but General Electric accepted the other basic provisions in the Wheeler agreement plus a somewhat broader product coverage and a provision that "requires the company to sell heavy equipment components to other manufacturers without discrimination; the company is not required to make the component available to other manufacturers, but if it sells to one, it must be willing to sell to all on equal terms and without tie-in sales."[48]

In consent judgments filed in November, 1962, with twelve other defendants, the settlements were generally in accordance with the General Electric pattern.[49] According to Walton and Cleveland: "At the beginning of 1963 fewer than half a dozen civil cases remained to be settled, and these were in the process of negotiation."[50]

The Benefits of the Episode in Review

I turn now to a brief recital of some of the benefits that came out of this episode in which the Tennessee Valley Authority had played an important part. In the first place, the electrical products conspiracy cases have served the useful purpose of reminding us that the task of maintaining a competitive economy is never ending. Agreements to restrain trade unreasonably, though long illegal, are profitable arrangements, and business firms in their pursuit of profit will ever be tempted to use this method if public policy is not continuously directed against such behavior. Alerted by what they found in electrical manufacturing, the antitrust authorities have extended their probes into the pricing policies of other industries, including aluminum cable, cement, copper and brass tube and pipe, industrial salt, and steel.[51] These probes have resulted in antitrust litigation in the case of cable, salt, steel, and tube and pipe. In regard to the indictment for price-fixing in the case of cable, it has been said that "data on TVA's experiences with identical bidding on such cable were used in connection with this case."[52]

In the second place, these cases have reiterated the value of reporting identical bids to the antitrust authorities for possible indication of anticompetitive behavior. President John F. Kennedy issued Executive Order No. 10936 on April 24, 1961, which directed the gathering and analysis of identical bids received by the federal and local levels of government. The Department of Justice has implemented this order. Under present regulations all agencies that buy for the federal government must inform the department of any identical bids on items costing more than $10,000. The department also invited purchasing officials for more than 2,000 state and local government units—ranging from states to school districts—to participate in a similar program for the regular reporting of bids on items costing over $1,000. These programs went into effect between July 15 and November 1, 1961.

The Department of Justice scans the data for evidence of price-fixing or bid-rigging and then occasionally makes a report to the President, Congress, interested state and local agencies, and the public, a report which includes the instances of identical bidding.[53] The primary objectives of the reporting program are to discourage identical bidding by publicizing the bidders and to provide leads for the Attorney General in ferreting out antitrust violations.[54]

Quite early in the program Attorney General Robert F. Kennedy said: "Many have told us they already are feeling the benefits . . . in considerably more competitive bidding."[55] More recently, following a survey undertaken in March, 1963, he reported: "The experience of the majority of the State and local agencies actively participating in the reporting program clearly indicates that a decline in identical bidding had been observed following issuance of the Executive order."[56] Still more recently his successor, Nicholas deB. Katzenbach, has said that "some State and local procurement officers have indicated that in their views the operation of the program has made competition for public business more vigorous."[57] In a resolution adopted unanimously at its 1963 annual meeting, the National Association of State Purchasing Officials urged continuation of and full participation in the program.[58]

Moreover, there has apparently been a decline in identical bidding at the federal level. Between 1962 and 1964, reports of federal government agencies show a 21.6 per cent decline in the volume of purchases affected by identical bidding.[59] Since reporting is mandatory for federal agencies, Attorney General Katzenbach believes that the reported reduction in identical bidding "appears to be a sound measure of the extent to which the Executive order has reduced the incidence of identical bidding."[60]

Although identical bidding seems to be declining, it has not been eliminated. Among the items on which TVA has received identical bids since the reporting program went into effect are carrier current equipment, condenser tubing, grinding balls, insulators, lightning arresters, power capacitor units, transformers, transmission cable,[61] and copper wire.[62] In a phone interview with a newspaper columnist, Paul Fahey, chief of TVA's purchasing division, said: "We get identical bids on the same old products—insulators, lightning arresters, steel. . . . But by and large I think a greater element of competition has entered the whole field of electrical equipment."[63]

Finally, it would appear that the antitrust action against collusion in the electrical products markets has been a factor tending to make competition more effective in these markets. Selling cartels have the purpose and effect of pegging prices at levels higher than full competition would allow. One would expect that their elimination would lead to lower price levels. Moreover, experience has shown that when prices are raised to artificially high levels through agreement an individual seller, under pressure to sell, may break the agreement and cut the price, precipitating retaliation and drastic price cuts, perhaps even leading to an unduly depressed level of prices.

Evidence available indicates that the electrical equipment industry is no exception to the general pattern. The prices of some electrical products began to drop during the course of the investigation, and after successful prosecution was assured, some prices dropped as much as 30, 40, or even 50 per cent.[64] Not all of these reductions have continued. In some cases prices have risen again to an intermediate level.

Over the longer run prices in the industry appear to be at lower levels than they were when the agreements were in operation. One financial journal reported in 1961 that prices for most generating and distribution apparatus were at the lowest levels since 1955.[65] In 1964 another business periodical reported that "the electrical equipment industry is in one of the sourest periods of business in its history. Prices are close to their lowest in years. . . ."[66] The price index for electrical equipment has declined slowly but steadily since 1959; in 1964 it was estimated to stand at 97, as compared to 100 in 1957–59.[67]

Of course these reductions in the price level of electrical equipment following the antitrust effort cannot be ascribed entirely to antitrust activity. No doubt, part of the decline should be attributed to increased competition from foreign producers in some markets. Further, it is possible that cost savings associated with changing technology have also been a factor in the decline in some instances.

Weaknesses in Contemporary Policy and Suggestions for Improvement

An analysis of the twenty product markets involved in the electric cases reveals that in some instances the number of rival sellers was and is extremely limited. In the case of meters, three firms accounted for the entire market; in the case of bushings and isolated phase bus, four suppliers constituted the market; and in the case of circuit breakers, five companies had 100 per cent of the market.[68] Moreover, since the criminal cases were closed, the number of producers of steam turbine-generators has been reduced from five to two; the two survivors were General Electric and Westinghouse,[69] with General Electric holding 60 per cent of the market.[70] When sellers are few, agreement becomes both easy to achieve and hard to detect. Although the thinness of demand and the economies of scale for some of these products may be such that there is room for only a few firms, it is desirable to have as many firms and as mixed a structure of large and small companies as the limiting factors will permit.

The cases once again demonstrated that it is often the fringe of small rivals that injects price competition into the market.[71] Actually, in some instances the high prices charged by the major suppliers induced entry, and the new entrants attempted to win a share of the market by undercutting the prices of their established larger rivals.[72] When the major suppliers saw their market shares slipping, they either tried to secure price uniformity through agreement, or they "met competition," carrying prices down to low levels. When they pursued the second course,[73] their smaller rivals, smarting under this rough treatment, became agreeable to collective price stabilization at higher levels.

General Electric's refusal to agree not to sell at "unreasonably low prices" where there was a "reasonable probability" that the low prices would have an anticompetitive effect points up one weakness in existing antitrust policy. Big conglomerate business apparently wants to retain the right to engage in commodity discrimination. In fact, a General Electric official thought the company was doing the competitive system a service when it resisted the government's request. Said he: "We stood our ground because we believed that our position was legally correct and the only possible position consistent with the national policy of maintaining fair and vigorous competition."[74] The power of the large conglomerate firm to control the prices charged by its smaller and less diversified rivals by practicing commodity discrimination is not adequately curbed by existing law. What to do about it remains a pressing problem for effective antitrust policy.

A second weakness in antitrust policy is revealed by the fact that mergers took place which apparently were not challenged by the antitrust authorities. In at least one instance a troublesome small price-cutter was acquired by one of the middle-sized firms, a participant in the concerted action.[75] Moreover, among the producers of insulators there was something of a merger movement.[76] The remedy lies in a closer scrutiny of mergers. Enforcement should be directed especially toward preventing the disappearance of any viable member of the competitive fringe through the merger route. Such action will help to maintain a mixed market structure of large and small firms, so necessary for effective competition.

It is common practice in the electrical equipment industry for manufacturers to quote prices on a delivered basis, a fact which points up a third area of concern. Typically, the sellers pursue a single-zone system of delivered pricing; that is, each seller quotes a price that prevails across the nation.[77] In his investigation of the identical bids which the Tennessee Valley Authority had received, Julian Granger noticed that "the bidders all quoted the same delivered price even though their plants are hundreds or thousands of miles apart."[78]

Use of single-zone pricing by the firms of an industry makes it difficult to achieve active price competition, especially when sellers are few. It reduces the uncertainty as to what price will prevail at any one delivery point and thus makes it easy to achieve uniformity of pricing through agreement. Spatial separateness of buyers and sellers and the possible complexity introduced by differing transport charges can be ignored. It would appear that a system of pricing f.o.b. plant without freight absorption would add an element of uncertainty that would make for more effective price competition. Possibly the antitrust authorities might consider requiring f.o.b. plant pricing without freight absorption as a remedy in those cases where concerted action and delivered pricing have both been involved.[79] As a punishment for conspiracy, firms might very well be deprived of their right to use a delivered pricing system.[80]

Professor William J. Baumol has objected to requiring f.o.b. pricing because he fears that "local monopoly" and higher prices might result.[81] In the present writer's judgment the "local monopoly" that may accompany the f.o.b. plant pricing is a rather innocuous form of monopoly, if one considers the competitive pressures that are present when spatially separated sellers compete by quoting prices f.o.b. plant without freight absorption.[82] Baumol also fears that large firms, instead of cutting prices to broaden their market area, might decentralize their production in numerous small and widely scattered plants, possibly losing economies of scale and raising prices.[83] To the extent that large firms followed such a policy they might well worsen their cost position relative to their intermediate or small rivals. Whether they could shift those higher costs to buyers would depend upon a number of factors, including what had happened to the cost position of the marginal firm and the pricing aggressiveness of the intermediate and small firms. In my judgment, Baumol's objections to f.o.b. pricing do not override the positive benefits on competition which such pricing could have when introduced into the market in the limited fashion proposed in this paper.

In the fourth place, the electric cases lend support to the view that the use of sealed bids and the interests of a competitive economy go together. Advertised procurement makes it easier for the small firm that emphasizes price to get a proportionally larger share of government contracts than its larger rivals.[84] As an official of a smaller firm said: "Smaller companies like our own have to depend to a very substantial degree upon sealed-bid business, because we may not have the standing with some of the buyers that some of our larger competitors have, and I suppose that from time to time companies like ours do attain substantial shares of that business, and I suppose that there may be others in the industry who feel that they are entitled to some share of that business."[85] General Electric, on the other hand, obtains only 6 per cent of its business through sealed bids and prefers to concentrate its efforts on the 94 per cent of its business where the customers are willing to pay a "higher price for a better quality product."[86] To the extent that smaller firms secure a disproportionately large share of government contracts, the effect of such awards on market structure is deconcentrating in itself.

Advertised procurement is superior to negotiated procurement of a competitive variety[87] because it places greater stress upon price and thus tends to discourage excessive quality and service competition. With sellers so often preferring to emphasize non-price forms of competition, it is helpful, from the standpoint of maintaining effective competition, to have purchasing procedures which turn attention to price. Recognizing these advantages, a congressional subcommittee concerned with defense procurement suggested: "Considering the great advantages that accrue . . . from competitive procurement and especially formally advertised procurement, it is recommended that a much greater effort be made along these lines."[88]

In deciding on the award in cases of identical bidding, procurement officials should be careful to choose those criteria that will tend to discourage unnecessary identical bidding in the future. In awarding contracts when bids are identical or when low bids are identical, the Tennessee Valley Authority has followed a procedure of giving preference to small business and to substantial surplus labor areas.[89] When two or more small business firms, both or all located in a substantial surplus labor area, give identical bids, the agency often puts their names in a hat and draws one of them.[90] In the case of cement, TVA has split the business among the identical low bidders or the identical bidders;[91] and in the case of mill steel products it has divided the purchase equally among all the bidders, including four that were identical and one that was not.[92] In the case of two contracts involving aluminum cable steel reinforced conductor, upon receipt of six identical bids, the Authority rejected the offers.[93] In the case of the one contract, it proceeded to negotiate with all of the firms and succeeded in getting one to cut its price. In the case of the other contract, the Authority re-advertised for bids and on the second try succeeded in getting a low bid.

Drawing names from a hat or sharing the business among all the identical bidders are not methods conducive to breaking a pattern of identical bidding because such procedures are exactly what the firms hope will be done if bids are identical. As the Attorney General of the United States had said: "These methods of resolving tie low bids tend to foster identical bidding since they eliminate the incentive for price competition by assuring the identical bidders that each will obtain an equal share of the public agency's business."[94]

As an alternative procedure, it has been suggested that in tie bids the award should go to the smallest company bidding, with total assets as the criterion of size.[95] As another alternative the award might be made to the firm that has the smallest share of the market. Although a buyer could not be expected to determine the market shares, the antitrust agencies might well develop and make available to purchasing agencies market share statistics on those products where identical bidding has been a frequent occurrence.

Finally, in the spring of 1961 the Department of the Interior, troubled by the fact that it was still receiving identical bids, introduced an anticollusive bidding clause in its invitations to bid, requiring each bidder to certify that his bid was arrived at independently.[96] Later, the department reported "a decline in the number of identical bids" and lower prices.[97] In June, 1961, the press reported that the Tennessee Valley Authority had begun to require all firms submitting bids to the agency to certify that the proposals were free of collusion, a requirement patterned after the one adopted by the Department of the Interior.[98] Toward the end of 1963 this procedure was generalized by administrative regulation to cover all bidders for federal government contracts.[99]

Moreover, the Antitrust Division of the Department of Justice is requiring "defendants seeking negotiated settlements of civil actions in which they are charged with collusive bidding, bid rigging or other pricing practices affecting public procurement, to agree to a provision which requires the filing of affidavits of non-collusion with bids submitted to public agencies."[100] As of December, 1964, there were in operation a total of twenty-nine such decrees affecting twenty-eight product categories.[101]

Concluding Comments

If the United States relies on competition as its primary weapon to moderate the discretionary use of economic power, it is always fitting that we have some of it. The Tennessee Valley Authority has made a contribution in this direction by sharing with congressional committees and enforcement agencies facts and clues gleaned from its purchasing activities which indicated that our competitive system was not working as well as it might. Thus the Authority helped uncover what turned out to be a rather far-reaching and thoroughgoing instance of price-fixing, bid-rigging, and market-sharing.

The Tennessee Valley Authority has been called a "pacesetter." It has served and continues to serve as a pacesetter in the establishment of economical rates for electricity. In the electrical products episode, the Authority has served as pacesetter in a new and different sense—in its willingness to cooperate with responsible officials in uncovering anticompetitive behavior in the economy and thus facilitating more effective enforcement of the antitrust laws.

References

1. *Business Week*, April 1, 1961, p. 67.
2. *Ibid.*, p. 62.
3. From the testimony of Paul Fahey, Director, Division of Materials, Tennessee Valley Authority, in U. S. Congress, Senate Subcommittee on Antitrust and Monopoly of the Committee on the Judiciary, *Hearings, Administered Prices*, 86th Cong., 1st Sess., 1959, Pt. 13, p. 6688. Cited hereafter as *Administered Price Hearings*, Pt. 13.

   Under formal advertising, "all bids in response to an invitation must be submitted to [TVA] in a sealed envelope, marked with the number of the invitation and the time that it is to be opened, which is set out in the invitation, and these bids are not opened until that time comes, and they are opened in public," *ibid.*
4. Calculated from data presented in Report of the Attorney General under Executive Order 10936, *Identical Bidding in Public Procurement*, July, 1962, p. 15, Table C; cited hereafter as First Report on *Identical Bidding in Public Procurement*. Second Report of the Attorney General under Executive Order 10936, *Identical Bidding in Public Procurement*, July, 1964, p. 3, Table B; cited hereafter as Second Report on *Identical Bidding in Public Procurement*. Third Report of the Attorney General under Executive Order 10936, *Identical Bidding in Public Procurement*, Feb., 1965, p. 3, Table B; cited hereafter as Third Report on *Identical Bidding in Public Procurement*. And Fourth Report of the Attorney General under Executive Order 10936, *Identical Bidding in Public Procurement*, Oct., 1965, p. 3, Table B; cited hereafter as Fourth Report on *Identical Bidding in Public Procurement*.
5. For a fuller treatment of this point, see Ronald H. Wolf, "Purchasing In a World of Identical Prices," *Journal of Purchasing*, II (Feb., 1966), 79–82.
6. *FTC* v. *Cement Institute*, 333 U.S. 683 (1948). Information in this paragraph is taken from Milton Britten's column, Knoxville *News-Sentinel*, May 23, 1959.
7. First Report on *Identical Bidding in Public Procurement*, p. 2.
8. From Fahey's testimony, *Administered Price Hearings*, Pt. 13, p. 6722.
9. First Report on *Identical Bidding in Public Procurement*, p. 3.
10. Information in this paragraph not otherwise referenced is taken from the statement of Lee Loevinger, Assistant Attorney General, Antitrust Division, Department of Justice, in U. S. Congress, House Sub-

committee of the Committee on Government Operations, *Hearings, Identical Bids to Public Agencies*, 87th Cong., 1st Sess., 1961, pp. 54–56.

11. *Ibid.*, pp. 56–57.
12. Information in this paragraph is taken from the Chattanooga *Times*, May 14, 1959.
13. For an interesting account of the details, see John G. Fuller, *The Gentlemen Conspirators* (New York: Grove Press, 1962), pp. 7–11, 21–30.
14. Granger's subsequent articles on TVA and identical bidding appeared on May 18 and 19.
15. Fuller, *op. cit.*, p. 30.
16. *Wall Street Journal*, Jan. 9, 1961.
17. Memphis *Press-Scimitar*, May 21, 1959.
18. *Business Week*, April 1, 1961, p. 63.
19. Fuller, *op. cit.*, p. 36.
20. *Business Week, loc. cit.*
21. Nashville *Tennessean*, July 1, 1959; Lee Linder's column, Knoxville *News-Sentinel*, March 12, 1961; and Knoxville *News-Sentinel*, July 21, 1959.
22. Clarence C. Walton and Frederick W. Cleveland, Jr., *Corporations On Trial: The Electric Cases* (Belmont, Calif.: Wadsworth Publishing Company, 1964), p. 32.
23. *Administered Price Hearings*, Pt. 13, pp. iii, 6686–6724.
24. *Ibid.*, pp. 6708–6709.
25. Fuller, *op. cit.*, p. 49.
26. Knoxville *News-Sentinel*, Feb. 17, 1960.
27. "Some Aspects of Antitrust Legislation and Its Enforcement," *Proceedings of the Thirty-Sixth Annual Conference of the Western Economic Association* (Salt Lake City, 1961), p. 8.
28. John Herling, *The Great Price Conspiracy* (Washington: Robert B. Luce, 1962), pp. 21–22.
29. *Ibid.*, p. 67.
30. Walton and Cleveland, *op. cit.*, p. 33. Literally, *nolo contendere* means, I do not wish to contest it.
31. Knoxville *News-Sentinel*, May 20, 1960.
32. Walton and Cleveland, *op. cit.*, pp. 34, 38.
33. *Ibid.*, p. 38.
34. *Business Week*, Dec. 3, 1960, p. 32.
35. The story of the electrical products conspiracies will not be retold here. The interested reader should consult the following: Fuller, *op. cit.*; Herling, *op. cit.*; Richard A. Smith, *Corporations in Crisis* (Garden City: Doubleday and Company, 1963), chaps. v and vi;

Walton and Cleveland, *op. cit.*; Richard A. Smith, "The Incredible Electrical Conspiracy," *Fortune*, April, May, 1961; John Brooks, "Annals of Business: The Impacted Philosophers," *New Yorker*, May 26, 1962; *U. S. News and World Report*, Feb. 27, 1961; Myron W. Watkins, "Electrical Equipment Antitrust Cases—Their Implications for Government and for Business," *University of Chicago Law Review*, Autumn, 1961; and *Wall Street Journal*, Jan. 9, 10, 12, and 13, 1961.

The Technical Library of the Tennessee Valley Authority also contains a bound volume entitled "TVA and Identical Bidding," which consists of a compilation of news stories, editorials, congressional debates, and testimony before a congressional subcommittee (Knoxville, July 12, 1961).

36. Walton and Cleveland, *op. cit.*, p. 39.
37. Department of Justice Release, March 14, 1961.
38. Knoxville *News-Sentinel*, July 27, 1962.
39. Information in this paragraph is taken from *ibid.*
40. Information on this settlement is taken from *ibid.*, April 28, 1963.
41. Information on the Westinghouse settlement is taken from *ibid.*, May 24, 1963.
42. Knoxville *Journal*, Sept. 1, 1965,
43. Information in this paragraph is drawn from *Business Week*, Sept. 4, 1965, p. 40; Knoxville *Journal*, Sept. 1, 1965; and *Time*, Sept. 10, 1965, p. 82.
44. Information in this paragraph is taken from Lee Linder's column, Knoxville *News-Sentinel*, March 12, 1961.
45. Information regarding the first three provisions of the decree is drawn from *Business Week*, May 27, 1961, p. 38.
46. Walton and Cleveland, *op. cit.*, p. 117.
47. Information in this paragraph is drawn from *ibid.*, pp. 117–122.
48. *Ibid.*, pp. 122–123.
49. Knoxville *News-Sentinel*, Nov. 16, 1962.
50. Walton and Cleveland, *op. cit.*, p. 119.
51. Knoxville *News-Sentinel*, March 3, 1961, and Sept. 13, 1962.
52. From Milton Britten's column, *ibid.*, Nov. 11, 1962.
53. Four reports have been issued: the first in July, 1962, the second in July, 1964, the third in Feb., 1965, and the fourth in Oct., 1965.
54. Third Report on *Identical Bidding in Public Procurement*, p. 30.
55. Knoxville *News-Sentinel*, Oct. 12, 1961.
56. Second Report on *Identical Bidding in Public Procurement*, p. 22.
57. Third Report on *Identical Bidding in Public Procurement*, p. 30.
58. *Ibid.*
59. Fourth Report on *Identical Bidding in Public Procurement*, pp. 2–3.

60. *Ibid.*, p. 20.
61. Knoxville *Journal*, Oct. 14, 1961, reporting a talk by Chairman Herbert D. Vogel at the University of Dayton in Ohio on "Competition and Administered Prices."
62. From Milton Britten's column, Knoxville *News-Sentinel*, Nov. 11, 1962.
63. *Ibid.*
64. Knoxville *Journal*, March 20, 1961, reporting a statement of Attorney General Robert F. Kennedy; and *Wall Street Journal*, Oct. 21, 1960.
65. *Financial World*, April 26, 1961, p. 10.
66. *Business Week*, Aug. 29, 1964, pp. 96–97.
67. *Ibid.*, p. 98.
68. Walton and Cleveland, *op. cit.*, p. 14, Table 1-1.
69. *Business Week*, Aug. 29, 1964, p. 102.
70. Walton and Cleveland, *op. cit.*, p. 24.
71. For examples, see U. S. Congress, Senate Subcommittee on Antitrust and Monopoly of the Committee on the Judiciary, *Hearings, Administered Prices*, 87th Cong., 1st Sess., 1961, Pt. 27, p. 16589 and Pt. 28, pp. 17472–17474, 17501, 17733–17734, 17837–17838. Cited hereafter as *Administered Price Hearings*, Pt. 27 or Pt. 28.
72. Raymond E. Gibson, "Antitrust and Moral Confusion," *Christian Century*, Nov. 8, 1961, p. 1333.
73. For examples, see *Administered Price Hearings*, Pt. 27, p. 17066 and Pt. 28, pp. 17398–17399, 17518, 17533–17535, 17859.
74. Knoxville *Journal*, Dec. 23, 1961.
75. *Administered Price Hearings*, Pt. 28, p. 17501.
76. *Administered Price Hearings*, Pt. 27, p. 16719.
77. *Administered Price Hearings*, Pt. 28, pp. 17435, 17624, 17739, 17799.
78. Knoxville *News-Sentinel*, July 21, 1959.
79. Vernon A. Mund has suggested another approach to getting at the problem of delivered pricing in his "theory of concurrent pricing." See his "Identical Bid Prices," *Journal of Political Economy*, LXVIII (April, 1960), 163–167, and his article in *Proceedings of the Thirty-Sixth Annual Conference of the Western Economic Association*, 1961, pp. 9–10.
80. There is precedent for such action. In cases involving abuse of the patent privilege, firms have been required to give up some of the rights usually associated with the patent privilege, such as the right not to license others or the right to charge any royalty that the market will bear. Instead, the courts have sometimes required compulsory licensing at a reasonable royalty.

81. William J. Baumol, "Identical Bidding and Uniform Pricing," (unpublished paper, dated May, 1961), p. 14.
82. For an incisive analysis of these pressures, see Frank A. Fetter, *The Masquerade of Monopoly* (New York: Harcourt, Brace, 1931), Chap. 20.
83. Baumol, *op. cit.*, p. 15.
84. *Administered Price Hearings*, Pt. 28, pp. 17472–17474.
85. *Ibid.*, p. 17535.
86. From Ralph J. Cordiner's testimony, *ibid.*, p. 17734.
87. Negotiated procurement may also be of a sole-source variety.
88. U. S. Congress, Subcommittee on Defense Procurement of the Joint Economic Committee, *Report, Impact of Military Supply and Service Activities on the Economy*, 88th Cong., 1st Sess., July, 1963, p. 4.
89. The detailed procedure followed by federal government agencies is set forth in Second Report on *Identical Bidding in Public Procurement*, pp. 16–17.
90. From Fahey's testimony, *Administered Price Hearings*, Pt. 13, p. 6689.
91. Knoxville *News-Sentinel*, Feb. 7, 1960, and April 1, 1960.
92. *Ibid.*, April 20, 1960.
93. Information on this episode is taken from the Knoxville *Journal*, July 25, 1963; July 26, 1963; Aug. 20, 1963; and Jan. 24, 1964.
94. Second Report on *Identical Bidding in Public Procurement*, p. 17.
95. Mund, in *Journal of Political Economy*, *op. cit.*, p. 168, credits the proposal to William Summers Johnson, Chief Economist, House Select Committee on Small Business.
96. U. S. Congress, Senate Subcommittee on Antitrust and Monopoly of the Committee on the Judiciary, *Hearings, Legislation to Strengthen Penalties Under the Antitrust Laws*, 87th Cong., 1st Sess., 1961, pp. 117–118.
97. *Ibid.*, p. 118.
98. Knoxville *Journal*, June 6, 1961, citing Paul Fahey.
99. Third Report on *Identical Bidding in Public Procurement*, p. 26.
100. Fourth Report on *Identical Bidding in Public Procurement*, p. 18.
101. Ibid., pp. 18–19, and Third Report on *Identical Bidding in Public Procurement*, pp. 26–28.

An Unfinished Task: A Socio-Economic Evaluation of the TVA Experiment

STEFAN H. ROBOCK is presently Professor of International Business and Director of the International Business Program at Indiana University. He holds the B.A. degree from the University of Wisconsin and the M.A. and Ph.D. degrees from Harvard University. During the period from 1940 to 1948 Dr. Robock held a number of government positions; from 1948 to 1954 he was Chief Economist for TVA; and during the period from 1954 to 1960 he held successive posts with the United Nations, Midwest Research Institute, and the Committee for Economic Development. His publications include "Regional and National Economic Development in India," "Nuclear Power and Economic Development in Brazil," and *Why Industry Moves South* (co-author).

The Tennessee Valley Authority as a pioneering experiment in integrated river-basin development has for a number of years been receiving the recognition and acclaim that it deserves. Its achievements in improving the social and economic welfare of the people of the Tennessee Valley region and the nation through regional resource development have become known throughout the world —and even to some extent within the United States. Thus it is appropriate on the occasion of TVA's thirtieth anniversary to pay tribute to the staff and alumni of the TVA and—more importantly—to the people of the Tennessee Valley who have contributed their support, enthusiasm, and direct efforts toward the success of this world-famous project.

Anniversary celebrations are usually devoted to eulogies and congratulations on achievements of the past, but they can also be appropriate occasions for recognizing unfinished tasks for future attention. Therefore, I have chosen to focus my remarks on an important unfinished task: that of making a comprehensive and objective socio-economic evaluation of the TVA experiment. As an economist, I am professionally embarrassed to admit that despite thirty years of rich TVA experience that can be studied, there does not exist a single broad scholarly work by an individual or group of economists evaluating the TVA as an approach to social and economic development. A few scholarly studies by sociologists and political scientists have been undertaken. But they are now quite old and have exploited only a small part of the magnificent opportunity provided by the TVA experience for making discoveries in the field of economic and social development, a field that now occupies much of the world's attention.

The unfinished task I have in mind is not to determine whether or not TVA has been a "success." There is adequate objective evidence to show that TVA has been a highly productive investment of federal funds, that the benefits to the nation have far exceeded the costs, and that the project has made a major contribution toward accelerating the development of the Tennessee Valley region. The source and nature of some of the continued domestic opposition to the TVA also provides impressive evidence that it has not been a failure. If TVA had been less efficient, less imaginative, and less successful, many of the forces of opposition who propose to sell or dismantle the TVA would be in favor of preserving it. They would be anxious to preserve TVA as a living example of the failure of government in the enterprise field.

Some Measure of Financial Success

The problem of measuring TVA's success by conventional cost-benefit techniques presents many fascinating professional challenges to economists and social scientists. And such crucial issues as benefits to whom and over what period of time need considerable clarification. But I will pass over the subject for the moment by simply asserting that current cost-benefit techniques are severely limited in providing the kind of broad evaluation that I am proposing. However, I am pleased to note that the cost-benefit studies of TVA have been broadened to include benefits to the nation as well as to the Tennessee Valley region. I am also pleased to note that new and non-traditional techniques have been used, such as demonstrating and quantifying the competitive effect of TVA low power rates in reducing the cost of electric power to millions of consumers outside of the TVA power service area and to the federal government itself.

If I had to choose one simple means of enlightening students and others on the financial benefits of the TVA to the federal taxpayer, a simple calculation of the savings to the federal government as a purchaser of power would be highly effective. For a number of years the federal government has been purchasing large quantities of electric power for the Atomic Energy Commission and other defense installations. The experience of the AEC more than a decade ago in negotiating with the private power industry to supply the AEC plant at Paducah, Kentucky, demonstrated specifically and dramatically that the taxpayer has been able to make a large saving by having TVA available as an alternative source of supply.

I do not know the total size of the power purchases by the federal government in the Tennessee Valley and adjoining region. But TVA itself sold 25 billion kilowatt hours in 1963 to the federal government. Assuming that total TVA and non-TVA purchases have been averaging about 30 billion kilowatt hours over the last decade, a saving of only 1 mill per kilowatt hour has meant a gain to the taxpayer of $300 million in the ten-year period. A saving of 2 mills per kilowatt hour, which is a reasonable estimate of the price reduction forced by TVA efficiency and competition, means that the taxpayer has saved a total of $600 million over the decade in national defense expenditures.[1] This, of course, represents only one of many national benefits that have flowed from the multipurpose activities of TVA.

The Need for a Comprehensive Socio-Economic Evaluation

Now back to my main theme. The task of evaluation that must be completed goes far beyond a calculation of success and failure in money terms. A socio-economic evaluation must examine in depth every dimension of the TVA experiment, so that the knowledge of why and how successes (and failures) occurred can be used to guide development efforts elsewhere in the United States and the world. President Johnson has given high priority to a war on poverty and to improving the economic and social welfare of Appalachia. The TVA experience could make invaluable contributions to both of these national programs if more were known about what worked and what didn't work in the Tennessee Valley and about the time horizons, the key stimuli, and the pattern of development associated with specific types of activities.

The direct benefits of the TVA through expanding the availability of electric energy; through experimentation with a low rate–high use policy in the distribution of electricity; through improving forestry, agricultural, and mineral resources; through fertilizer research; and through flood control and river navigation are impressive and should not be minimized. But the benefits that can result from making wise use of the full TVA experience in regional and resource development elsewhere in the United States and the world would completely overshadow this direct welfare contribution.

During the next forty to fifty years, several hundred billion dollars will be invested in integrated river-basin projects throughout the world, according to a recent estimate by a panel of United Nations experts.[2] And even more capital and human effort will be invested domestically and internationally in national and regional development activities which could benefit from a better understanding of the TVA experience. The engineering aspects of river and other types of development are relatively well understood. But the economic, social, and administrative dynamics of development are much less understood than, for example, the problem of sending a man to the moon.

Unfortunately, in my view, it has been easier in the United States to obtain resources and priority for research on space and moon shots than for research on the problems of economic and resource development. In support of physical science research, it may be demonstrated that such research is more manageable than the complex problems of social and economic development; controlled experiments can be undertaken and the time horizons for observing results are relatively short.

But I will argue that a socio-economic evaluation of the TVA experience is feasible and that many favorable conditions exist for such research. TVA was established long before the issues of development became internationally popular, and it now has three decades of experience that can be studied to advantage. Another favorable factor is that TVA's main activities have been localized in a relatively small geographical area. Also, an unusually large amount of data is available on past and present trends in the regional and national environment in which TVA has operated.

There is one other general point before I turn to a more specific discussion of the approach and content of the evaluation that I think must be undertaken. TVA has long emphasized that its experience cannot be duplicated identically in other areas of the United States and the world. The TVA experiment combines a set of ideas and institutions, a specific regional and national environment, and a certain time period. These various components must be separated for application in other areas, other institutional settings, and other time periods. The actual shape of the TVA itself would have been different if the project had been initiated in 1928, when a TVA bill was passed by the Congress but vetoed by President Coolidge, or if the project had been initiated after World War II. In other words, there are many special circumstances that explain the particular pattern of institutions and results which emerged and flourished in the Tennessee Valley.

My argument for a comprehensive socio-economic evaluation of the TVA experience can be summarized as follows:

1. Social and economic development in the future will occupy a large and probably increasing share of the nation's and the world's attention and resources. The TVA experience can provide valuable guidance for these efforts.

2. The form of the TVA experiment cannot be duplicated exactly elsewhere, but unusually favorable conditions exist for separating and analyzing the many components of the TVA experience so that it can be applied in other situations.

3. The conventional cost-benefit studies have serious limitations in providing guidance for other development activities. They focus on quantifying results in monetary terms at particular points in time, rather than on identifying cause and effect and the patterns over time that were followed in achieving specific results from specific development activities.

A Possible Approach

Now let us consider the approach and content of the evaluation research that should be undertaken. It must be recognized that the social and economic effects of a river-basin project depend upon the interaction of new physical facilities, institutions, and technology on the people, resources, institutions, political units, and development potentials of the region in which the project is installed, and on the nation of which the region is a part. Predicting the economic and social effects of a given investment in a resource-development project is much more difficult and tenuous than predicting the effects of a new industrial plant.

Evaluation studies, therefore, must describe in detail the regional and national environment within which the river-basin project has been operating. They should also identify specifically the ways in which the new facilities and programs, or various combinations of the new facilities and programs, have stimulated or supported the actions of individuals and institutions in achieving higher levels of income and employment and other specified social goals. And all of this analysis must be traced on a time dimension so that the sequence of events can be determined.

Evaluation studies must also identify and specify the complete range of complementary or secondary initiatives, policies, investments, and institutions which were required to translate the new physical facilities into economic and social results. Again, a time sequence for complementary actions must be related to specific aspects of the river-basin project.

Let me illustrate a possible pattern for evaluation research by referring to a study I prepared in 1963 for the United Nations Conference on the Application of Science and Technology for the Benefit of the Less Developed Areas. This study, entitled "Integrated River Basin Development and Industrialization: The Tennessee Valley Experience,"[3] was based largely on research conducted while I was on the staff of TVA. However, it does not have behind it as much basic investigation as would be justified by the importance of the subject. As the title implies, my effort was to evaluate, on the basis of the TVA experience, the role of river-basin projects in stimulating and supporting industrialization.

Many areas of the United States and virtually all of the underdeveloped countries aspire to achieve higher levels of industrialization. And installation of river-basin projects is one of the paths being followed to induce industrial development. A thorough and detailed understanding, therefore, of the effect of TVA activities—extending over thirty years—on industrialization in the region and the nation can be of inestimable value. Such knowledge applied in other areas, as well as in future Tennessee Valley activities, can make more effective the impact of such projects. Such knowledge can make expectations more realistic and even avoid a waste of scarce resources where potentials are not promising.

Development of a General Theory. The first step in such an evaluation is to develop an hypothesis or a general theory that embraces the scope of the specific inquiry. In this specific case, the general theory tried to answer the following question: what is the causal relationship between the integrated river-basin projects and industrialization? And my answer was as follows:

1. River-basin projects are only partial approaches to industrial development. They generally have no direct control over many activities necessarily involved in a full development program such as taxes, fiscal policies, transportation rates and policies, tariffs and foreign trade, labor-management laws, public investment in schools, hospitals, roads, and educational policies.

2. The main influence of river-basin projects is on the physical supply and cost conditions of certain resources in a region. The rate at which the improved resource situation is translated into new and expanded industrial activity will depend upon demand factors usually outside the control of the river-basin project. Furthermore, improved physical availability is not a sufficient condition for industrial development.

Markets must exist for the specific resources being improved. Business entrepreneurship, government or private, must be active. And complementary policies and activities by other government and private agencies are essential. Furthermore, depending upon the locational characteristics of new enterprises, the industrialization stimulated by the improved resource situation may be most efficiently located outside of the river valley region.

3. The large investment required for a river-basin project and its multiplier effect does not necessarily create a self-generating regional demand for resources. In a predominantly agricultural region, a large share of the direct impact of the investment expenditures is likely to be outside the basin and even outside the country. The geography of the investment impact will depend

upon the specific composition of the project and the productive facilities of the region and the country. Expenditures for construction labor and many local services will generally mean increased income and employment in the region. But the substantial expenditures for generators, turbines, and other electrical, mechanical, and construction equipment will normally go to the developed regions of the foreign countries which produce this equipment.

Description of Trends. After developing a general theory of causal relationships, a second step in such an evaluation is to describe in detail the trends that have occurred in the valley region in the specific field of inquiry. For example, in my own inquiry, the task was to describe the amount and type of industrialization that had occurred in the Tennessee Valley region, the greater Southeast, and the nation as a whole. A summary of the results of this phase may be of interest.

1. Industry expanded more rapidly in the Tennessee Valley than in the nation as a whole or in the larger Southeast region. Manufacturing employment increased from 222,000 in 1929 to 486,000 in 1960, a gain of 119 per cent as compared to 101 per cent in the Southeast and 55 per cent in the nation. Manufacturing wages and salaries grew from slightly more than $200 million to almost $2 billion from 1929 to 1960, an increase of 807 per cent as compared to 720 per cent in the Southeast and 443 in the nation.

2. Industry expanded much more rapidly than agriculture in the Tennessee Valley, both as a source of employment and of income. In 1930, the Valley region had four farm workers for every factory worker. But by 1960 factory workers outnumbered farm workers by a margin of almost two to one, and manufacturing was providing almost three times the income from agriculture.

3. In terms of new jobs, the most important growth industries in the Valley region were apparel, food, chemicals, electrical machinery, furniture, primary metals, leather, non-electrical machinery, pulp and paper, and transportation equipment. These ten groups provided 80 per cent of the new jobs created between 1939 and 1958, the years for which detailed industry data are available.

4. The industrialization pattern differed for the various time

periods. From 1939 to 1947, covering the World War II period, the basic materials industries of chemicals, primary metals, and lumber were the leaders in expansion. In the postwar period, however, consumer goods industries came to the fore in terms of new manufacturing jobs, and the apparel and food industries accounted for 50 per cent of the employment increase in manufacturing. It is significant to note that "value added" expanded rapidly in chemicals, primary metals, and rubber products even though employment in metals and rubber showed little or no increase in the latter period. This reflects continued gains in productivity through heavy capital investment and automation.

5. The geographical distribution of industrial expansion within the Valley region is of special interest to proponents of rural industries and opponents of urbanization, because manufacturing activity continued to be heavily concentrated in the urban counties.

Identification of Causal TVA Programs. Having developed a general understanding of the causal relationships between a river-basin project and industrialization trends, the third step was to identify and describe in some depth the key TVA programs that were likely to have influenced industrialization. The direct programs were grouped into three categories: (1) physical resources improvement; (2) technical studies and research; and (3) planning and industrial promotion activities. A fourth and indirect factor was the over-all expansion of the regional income and the regional market, which has an important stimulus for some types of industries.

Establishing Cause and Effect. The fourth step of the analysis was the most precarious—to establish a cause-and-effect relationship between TVA programs and specific industrialization projects in the region. Nevertheless, it was possible to make an estimate—by examining the locational characteristics of expansions and new Valley industries—that TVA programs were a significant factor behind one-third of the new industrial jobs and at least one-half of the increased value added by industry. And because of the capital-intensive nature of most of the TVA-oriented industries, this group accounted for well over half of the total new manufacturing investment in the Valley.

The specific industries attracted by TVA programs were: chemicals (including industrial chemicals), man-made fibers, and fertilizers; primary metals such as aluminum and ferro alloys; forest products such as pulp and paper and paperboard; electrical machinery; and food processing. The bulk of the resources-oriented industries are producing for a national rather than a regional market, and they have attracted relatively few final-products industries to the Tennessee Valley. The chemicals, primary metals, and paper industry plants are highly capital intensive and required investments of from $30,000 to $70,000 per worker as compared to an over-all average for the region of less than $8,000 per worker. In the Calvert City, Kentucky, area, in which an extensive industrial complex has developed since 1948, each industrial job required a total industrial plus power investment of almost $90,000.

Some Implications. An evaluation of TVA and industrialization such as I have briefly described covers only one of the many dimensions of the TVA experiment. It represents only a beginning study in the industrialization field. For example, a field survey completed some years ago of industries that had located on Tennessee River sites revealed that a large number of plants made no use whatever of the river. It also indicated that of those whose location was influenced by the river, more were attracted by the availability of a large, dependable supply of industrial water than by access to river transportation.

Yet despite its limitations, the example cited should clearly demonstrate the great value of TVA evaluation studies for development programs elsewhere in the nation and the world. Some of the conclusions from the industrialization study applicable in other areas are the following:

1. Integrated river-basin projects can stimulate a significant amount of industrialization. However, such projects involve massive investment and require a long period for producing industrialization results. The directly induced industrialization is likely

to be of a basic-industry type and highly capital intensive. Therefore, it must be cautioned that river-basin projects are neither a cheap nor a quick way to create industrial employment.

2. The mere increase in the physical availability of resources does not automatically create new industries. Therefore, the composition of the resource development and other components of an integrated river-basin project must be guided by national and international market demands. In many foreign areas this can be accomplished by integrating the planning of river-basin projects in the early stages with national economic development planning.

3. Complementary programs and projects beyond the normal scope of integrated river-basin projects are absolutely essential to secure aid and significant industrialization results. Such activities may involve technical surveys of resources, industrial process research, land use planning, and manpower training programs.

4. A final application of the TVA experience relates to an intangible matter. Probably the greatest contribution of a river-basin project to industrialization and economic development in general can be building regional institutions and providing a new growth perspective to an area. An integrated river-basin project as a dramatic regional venture can be an invaluable framework for mobilizing the human and institutional resources of a region for new, high levels of development. On the other hand, if such projects are not soundly conceived and viewed in proper perspective they can siphon off the productive energies of an economy toward the undesirable end of "monument building."

I have taken considerable time to describe the procedure and results of my own effort to evaluate the industrialization effects of the TVA experiment. The actual conclusions of this study may be of interest themselves. But my principal purpose has been to demonstrate that it is feasible to undertake evaluation studies and that the results can be of significant operational importance in many regions of the country and nations of the world. The usual objection one hears when evaluation studies are proposed is that it is not feasible to identify cause and effect and to isolate specific features of a complex and comprehensive economic and social development experience. I am attempting to argue—with some persuasion, I hope—that evaluation studies can and should be undertaken.

Such studies, of course, can never be definitive or complete. Yet the results can be substantial and significant. In my study, for example, the industrialization I have identified as TVA-oriented is a minimum rather than a maximum. But the incomplete results are significant and operationally useful. And if a larger effort had been devoted to the project, the results would have been even more useful.

Unfilled Needs

What are some of the other evaluation studies that should be undertaken? There are many. The activities in fertilizer research and in stimulating more effective fertilizer use should be evaluated in relation to social and economic development in the Tennessee Valley and in other regions of the country. Both the impact on agriculture and on industry should be investigated. The electric power program has many dimensions for investigation. What are the implications to economic and social development of pricing policies, of technical and distribution innovations, of purchasing policies, of the contribution of a power program in building local institutions that can undertake industrial and agricultural development?

A wide range of evaluation studies is called for in the field of agricultural development, forest resources, water sanitation, fish and wildlife, public health, recreation, physical planning, minerals research, water transportation, and others. In all of these areas, a general hypothesis of the relationship of these activities to economic and social development should be articulated. The general and specific economic and social trends should be determined. And the TVA programs must be related on a cause and effect basis to the events that have unfolded.

In all cases, of course, the failures as well as the successes should be studied. One of the purposes of such evaluations is to define the limitations as well as the potentials of the integrated river-basin project. Also, the evaluations must describe in depth the environment in which the programs have been applied and the external or non-TVA forces that were influential.

In the field of fertilizer use and agricultural development, for example, it is important to relate TVA activities to national farm policies, to the work of non-TVA institutions such as the universities and farm credit agencies, and to study the social characteristics of the farmer. Development activities which have been successful in an area where farmers are literate will have to be modified or supplemented when used in areas such as Bolivia or Afghanistan, where most of the peasants cannot read or write.

Why have so few evaluation studies of the TVA experience been completed? Several possible reasons can be suggested. The most important explanation may be found in the primitive state of the arts for evaluation research in the social science field. The available theoretical work on economic and social development is quite unsatisfactory and evaluation techniques are poor. In large part, the primitive state of the arts reflects a serious lag on the part of social scientists in becoming interested in development problems. It also reflects a public policy failure to provide strong incentives for attracting social scientists to this type of work.

Another explanation may be the confusion that exists between cost-benefit studies and operationally oriented evaluation research. The emphasis on cost-benefit techniques arises from a unique institutional situation in the United States. In 1936, the Federal Flood Control Act stated that the federal government should sponsor flood control projects "if the benefits to whomsoever they may accrue are in excess of the estimated costs. . . ." Through practice or legislation the cost-benefit criterion has been extended to almost all water projects and to many other public services. The principal use of the results is to enlighten political decision-making and in some cases to prevent traditional "pork barrel" projects. Cost-benefit studies can assist in evaluations because they attempt to identify specific results from specific programs. But evaluation studies, as I have previously emphasized, must go far beyond this first step.

A third explanation may lie within the frequently stormy history of the Tennessee Valley Authority itself. In its early months, TVA had many social scientists on its staff. But very soon the planning of the physical facilities began to occupy more of the energy and time of management personnel than did the broader economic and social considerations. This happened partly because the construction program was demanding of energy and time and partly because the directors found it easier to agree on engineering matters than on social and economic considerations.

There has been a recurring awareness within TVA of the need for a comprehensive socio-economic evaluation of the TVA experience. And from time to time, work in this direction has been initiated. In some cases the evaluation work has been interrupted by an urgent need to have the social science staff work on operational problems, including the preparation of responses to strong attacks on TVA. In one other case that is well known to me personally, an economics staff that had been assembled after years of effort was quickly lost to the agency because of strong controversy among members of the Board of Directors. Probably the time has come for TVA to make another effort in this direction and take the lead in seeing that such an evaluation effort is undertaken and completed.

This leads to my final question. "How should the unfinished task be undertaken?" And here I would recommend that an evaluation program should be undertaken by a research group located outside of the TVA. It has been true of most operating organizations that it is difficult if not impossible to protect an evaluation staff from the pressures of operating problems. Highly qualified personnel are required for such imaginative and pioneering work. And such quality of personnel is always in demand for high-priority, immediate tasks if they are part of the operating agency.

Also, it is difficult for an organization to evaluate itself in an objective way. There is an understandable reluctance to discover failures, even though a large number of failures in economic development work, as in product research within a commercial firm, are to be expected and may even be a sign of daring and imagination. There is an inevitable bias that comes from being part of the activity being evaluated.

A thorough evaluation is one of the major unfinished tasks related to the TVA experiment. It offers an unparalleled opportunity for expanding the contribution of the TVA project to the aspirations of the people of the world for a better life. I hope that there is a will and a way to meet this need and to seize this opportunity.

References

1. It is possible that the *net* saving to the federal government was less than the amount estimated above because of offsetting federal income tax payments by the private utilities. On the other hand, TVA has made a profit in supplying this demand and *all* of the TVA profit has become an asset of the United States. Another real possibility is that the lower prices for electric energy represent lower costs rather than lower profits.
2. United Nations, *Integrated River Basin Development, Report by a Panel of Experts* (E/3066) (New York: United Nations, 1958), p. 8.
3. *Science, Technology, and Development; United States Papers Prepared for the United Nations Conference on Application of Science and Technology for Benefit of Less Developed Areas*, Volume IV, *Industrial Development* (Washington: U. S. Government Printing Office, 1962–63). 12 v.

Toward More Realistic Assumptions in Regional Economic Development

GILBERT BANNER received the B.S., M.S., A.M., and Ph.D. degrees from the University of Michigan. He has been Assistant Professor of Economics at the University of Tennessee since 1957. Dr. Banner is the author of several articles in the areas of conservation and resource development.

Should TVA consider its experimental and pioneering work completed and remain simply the manager of the river and the power complex it has created? Or should TVA still consider as its mandate the continuous job of regional social and economic development?

These questions are asked because TVA's activities do not speak for themselves. TVA has been criticized for lack of effort in regional economic development, and its programs for advancing or stimulating economic development appear inadequate for current regional problems. To many critics, TVA seems primarily an operating agency, engineering-oriented in its activities. To some of these critics, TVA does too little in the area of educating the public and too little in the coordination of state and local programs aimed at economic growth.

What can a regional planning agency do today within the boundaries set by the existing private market economy, political subdivisions, and federal programs? A regional authority could explore current and potential regional problems and coordinate planning activities that affect the region. A regional authority could have broad powers to inventory resources and plan for their development. It could have authority to coordinate transportation and land uses and guide the growth of a desirable industrial mix. It could buy lands, or reserve them, to protect resources and to channel development. It could set boundaries for free enterprise entrepreneurs by using zoning and other tools of the police power to minimize social costs and give direction to economic change.

TVA has believed that these planning and implementing powers belong to the states and that TVA's responsibility is to help the states assume and use these powers. Over the years TVA has accepted the responsibility of helping states and local governments create the necessary planning and implementing organization and to assist in coordinating their activities in the region.

The TVA Act gave specific authority to TVA for some of these planning and implementing functions on the river. TVA has planned specific projects related to the control of the river and its tributaries and to energy production. It has helped private industry to locate on lands under its control on the river. It has inventoried natural resources in the region.

TVA has not asked for additional powers as a regional planning agency. Its role has been to inventory natural resources and to offer coordinating services to existing agencies of federal, state, and local government. Its regional planning has been in the nature of providing general guidelines for education and coordination. In this limited role, TVA has had large impact on the direction and rate of change in the region. It has helped in the creation of state and local planning agencies and in the work they have done.

It is generally accepted that TVA has been a success in the development of a multi-unit, multipurpose river system. In this sense, TVA holds itself up as a model of orderly, integrated resource development for the rest of the world to follow.[1] TVA has been less successful in the development of the land resources in its geographic area and still less so in bringing about the social and economic changes required for economic development. TVA measures the extent of its effect on social and economic development by comparing average income and other aggregate figures of TVA counties and states with those of the counties and states of other areas. These figures, compiled from counties that have heterogeneous land and economic characteristics, can be misleading. The atomic energy complex of Oak Ridge, a federal project, and the surrounding coal areas of Anderson County add up to a high county average, but the figures do not show the redistributive effect of this large government project nor the social failure of our private economic system in the depressed coal lands. The figures do not tell what is due to TVA; they do not tell what might have occurred without TVA. The depressed areas which pull down the averages are not the fault of TVA. Rates of income increase, implying that the poor are catching up to the rich, may be misleading. The poor may be improving at a faster rate than the rich, but still be at a low level. Averages, unfortunately, hide the fact that some poor have not improved and, relatively speaking, are poorer today. The averages may conceal the plight of the depressed areas. TVA can be criticized for its lax use of these aggregate figures and similar "public relations" comparisons.

Criticism of TVA

TVA is criticized regarding its role in regional economic development. These criticisms must be reviewed in historical context before suggestions can be offered for current and future TVA policy and activity.

For evaluation purposes, we can ask of TVA as we can of any organization: Were the problems for which the organization was created fully understood? Do the problems still exist? Are the organization's powers and administrative machinery adequate to solve these problems? Are the policies and programs the organization has established appropriate for the job? If the problems are changing, has the organization the flexibility to adjust to these changes?

Often in critical evaluation the idealist compares the results achieved to ideal objectives, while the administrator assesses the results achieved in the face of political and other restraints. The administrator may have to compromise in order to accomplish something in the desired direction; and if he accomplishes that which he thought possible, he considers his work a success. The idealist may interpret the same results as failure.

There are two kinds of TVA critics: those who assume that TVA should not now exist or should not have been created, and those who assume that TVA was and still is ideologically legitimate but is not doing all that it should. The former oppose TVA for many reasons: as a symbol of the federal government's interference in the states' responsibilities, as an intrusion into the domain of private enterprise, or as a threat to other federal agencies and programs. Some feel that although its original establishment was legitimate, TVA is already too big, or has gone into programs not originally intended. We are not concerned with this type of critic in this paper. We are interested only in asking whether

TVA can do a better job in the area of economic and social development than it has done previously.

Constructive criticism of TVA may be separated into two areas: criticism of its failure to establish programs to meet all its original objectives, *i.e.*, not doing certain things at all; and criticism of the adequacy of established programs, *i.e.*, not doing well what it is attempting to do.

To some critics, TVA's failures are those of omission: TVA has not attempted programs that could well have been successful. Are such "failures" only in the minds of critics? That is, are they not failures at all? Do such complaints represent unwarranted criticisms for TVA's neglecting to do what could not have been done? The author believes that TVA has been considered a failure in the area of regional economic development largely because the great expectations of accomplishment in this area were unrealistic.

TVA was given a general mandate to act on regional economic problems. Apparently, during the course of TVA's development, the kind of social and economic programs that might better have solved economic problems would have received neither local support nor congressional sanction. On the one hand, it might be argued that, recognizing its limitations, TVA never asked for funds for these specific programs. The Authority can be criticized for not indicating more forcefully that without adequate national programs it could do little to cope with the social and economic problems of the region. If TVA had emphasized publicly the nature and magnitude of these problems as they were recognized (assuming TVA had recognized their magnitude), some of the current criticism might have been avoided. On the other hand, it is possible that TVA did not recognize the magnitude of the problems and spoke in good faith of the adequacy of its activities in the realm of social and economic improvement.

Early TVA Policy and Assumptions on Economic Development

In this paper we will examine early assumptions made by TVA concerning the role of agriculture, navigation, and power in economic development. These assumptions underlay policy and programs for solving economic and social problems of the region. Today it appears that some of these assumptions were not realistic in terms of the problems that existed in TVA's early days. In any case, with changing economic conditions some of these assumptions are clearly not appropriate today. If policy and programs can be based on more realistic assumptions, TVA may continue successfully to experiment in regional economic development. Otherwise, TVA will be, as some say it has been for some time, merely an operating agency for a successful experiment in multipurpose river management.

TVA early established an administrative policy to decentralize many of its activities, a policy of operating with existing agencies at the "grass roots." TVA assumed that it could move no faster than these agencies and the people of the region would permit. It was committed to education through local channels and could only help if help were acceptable to local people. This policy of decentralization was based on the ideological assumption of the value of democratic action, as well as on the political judgment that TVA could only exist on these grass-roots terms.

By 1952, Norman Wengert, in his study, *Valley of Tomorrow*,[2] indicated that TVA policies and programs were already set. More effective social and economic measures would have required programs and funds that Congress would not have given. As a result, more active land-use programs and more definite economic development activities were not requested. TVA was not in a position to do much about impoverished areas if public responsibility was not recognized on a national level. TVA could be no more "socialistic" or "welfare-oriented" than the rest of the country permitted it to be through congressional interest in these matters and control of appropriations.

TVA was created when the country was in a depression. Parts of the agricultural South had been depressed before this time. The land-use practices and agricultural patterns were hard on the land and on the people. In other parts of the country in previous periods, when agricultural practices were no longer economic, the people moved on, leaving relatively few people in low-income land uses. Now, large numbers found themselves in a depressed condition with no low-cost lands open. This was true for a substantial portion of the TVA region.

TVA was created to control and develop the river and to improve the social and economic conditions of the region, and thereby the nation. It also had a munitions and fertilizer facility to operate. The objectives and means of controlling and harnessing the river and operating the fertilizer facility were relatively clear-cut; those for regional economic development were not spelled out. At that time there was little to spell out. Regional development theory and regional planning was then in its infancy. The economics profession had little to offer in the way of a theory of economic growth. TVA assumed that automatic economic growth would occur as the unused resources in the region were developed. This assumption was implicit in the classical economics of the day.

TVA assumed that opening up the region to low-cost river navigation would create markets for agricultural and manufactured products and that the agricultural economy was potentially sound, needing only a change from cash row crops. It was hoped that widespread fertilizer use would bring about this change and create a new type of agriculture as competitive and prosperous as agriculture in other parts of the nation. It was assumed that the people who had low-income farms would become more efficient or would find other farms that were economic units. If they left full-time farming, they would remain on the land as part-time farmers or rural residents with non-agricultural income sources in the new jobs created by industrial development. Given these assumptions, the physical development of the river resources as one major effort, and the fertilizer program to put low-income agriculture back on its feet as the other, seemed to be comprehensive. Cooperation with the existing federal agencies and their national programs in the region was adequate.

Just as poor land use and resultant soil erosion were not an immediate threat to TVA reservoir life, and land programs were not imperative for the success of the river development, so the possible unemployment due to changes in agriculture did not appear to be an immediate problem. The demonstration farm program in cooperation with the agricultural extension service was thought to be sufficient to carry out the required rural changes in resource use.

TVA recognized that education and training were necessary to create a labor force from rural people, but no special programs for this purpose seemed to be required. In current economic terms, the possibility of structural unemployment and depressed areas in a full-employment economy was not recognized. Therefore, there was thought to be no need for machinery to help the poor farmers who could not get adequate income from their land nor any machinery to help get them off the land. It seemed reasonable to assume that the fertilizer program, the key to agricultural change, together with flood control, navigation, and power would automatically improve the region. And as the national economy got back on its feet, the region, with the assets of a controlled river and rejuvenated agriculture, would automatically catch up with the rest of the country.

Relative Failure of TVA in Economic Development

It was soon evident that the assumptions about agriculture were not valid. Subsistence areas of agriculture were not capable, unassisted, of adjusting to better uses of land. People who were not needed on the land did not readily find jobs off the land. The various national agriculture programs to help low-income farmers did not improve to any great extent the low-income farm areas and did seem to freeze people on the land with low incomes. No regional program could have been carried out when there was no nationwide program to get people off the land.

The hoped-for social and economic "catching up to the rest of the country" that was to result from TVA programs did not occur for the entire region. Industrialization did not automatically follow power production, and areas of unemployment did not automatically disappear as the country reached higher levels of economic activity. Navigation did not prove to be as important to industrial location as had been expected. Sections of agriculture were not just temporarily sick; they were chronically ill.

What changes have occurred in the national economy since TVA's inception to make the original assumptions relative to automatic regional growth less valid than they might have been in the beginning?

First, navigation did not open the area to development as anticipated, because the transportation revolution in motor carriers and the construction of new roads altered the locational importance of waterways to industry and commerce. Highway location and other location factors became more important than water transportation.

Second, in an industrial society power is only one of many locational factors for industry. Only a few industries locate primarily on the basis of power needs. Raw materials, skilled labor, research and development facilities, and markets are often more important.[3] Where other factors are favorable, power has been produced when it was needed. Furthermore, as a result of technological advances in fuel and power transmission, industry does not have to locate at the source of fuel or power. Oil and gas pipelines and long-distance electric power transmission have increased locational flexibility with regard to power, making other locational factors more important. Since TVA's inception, other low-cost public power developments have been created elsewhere in the country, and there has been growth in the realm of private power. The trend in industrial location has been for the largest increase in new jobs to be in the already industrialized areas.

Finally, in agriculture, irrigated lands and new technology increased agricultural productivity. Less productive or poorly organized lands, on which it was difficult to capitalize and use the newer ideas, were not competitive. The farmers in large areas of low-income or part-time farming were, in fact, unemployed. In addition, areas that had been dependent on mining found themselves with large numbers of unemployed as changes took place in the coal industry. Many unemployed farmers and miners did not leave the land and the region. Those who did leave often added to the number of unemployed in the urban areas. Those who remained were the rural unemployed. The agricultural subsidy programs did not help these poor people.

From the vantage point of hindsight, it would appear that TVA did not adjust its philosophy or programs to these emerging changes. Several explanations are possible. Perhaps TVA did not see the implications of these national changes for the TVA area. It is also possible that TVA policy and programs were too rigid to permit adjustments. It might be that TVA's apparent ineffectiveness was the result of the lack of sympathy and funds from the Congress and administration during the Eisenhower years.

In the beginning, the farm unit had been chosen as the logical starting point for total resource planning. In a rural economy, this was a reasonable choice. TVA experimented on small watersheds, an area of farm units, controlling the water system while helping individual farms adjust farming practices in the interest of higher incomes. However, the rural area is only a part of the economy and part of a region's resources.

In the last few years, TVA has expanded its activities in support of small watershed associations, citizen organizations through whose efforts it is hoped that local people will examine their total resources and problems and come up with solutions. TVA helps the watershed associations in making a resource inventory, recognizing problems, developing solutions, and in pointing out existing state and federal assistance programs. With TVA's help, local organization and participation results in local solutions that are locally accepted. This is grass-roots democracy in action.

These watershed associations, based on county and municipality representation, are moving toward becoming resource development authorities with statutory powers and state financial support to solve problems of economic and social development. The potential of the small-watershed program in economic development and its role as part of a larger economic development program will be discussed more fully later.

Policy Choices Open to TVA

We have assumed that TVA could do very little about problems that were the result of changes and trends in the national economy as long as the federal government assumed no responsibility on a national level. In the last few years, the federal government has accepted this responsibility with such programs as "community facilities," "urban renewal," "area redevelopment," and the poverty programs. In light of these national programs, what can TVA do now in furthering regional development that it could not do before?

1. TVA might increase the tempo of tributary-stream control and development, an extension of its engineering activities on the smaller tributaries.

2. TVA might put greater emphasis on its coordinating role in assisting the states and local governments to create the planning and implementing machinery required for increasing economic development in a regional context.

3. TVA might, through the small-watershed programs, catalyze, expedite, and coordinate the development of local resources and take advantage, when possible, of the federal programs within its borders.

The expanding federal programs with centralized administrative machinery, operating through regional, state, and local political units, will require much coordination if grass-roots action is to lead to effective total resource development. Here, there is much for TVA to do. It will be a big job to coordinate all the aid available so that it fits a larger objective or direction for the region. However, although the federal programs proliferate, the TVA staff is short of trained people to do the required job of guiding, coordinating, planning, and analyzing.

We originally asked whether TVA has a choice: Can it do much in the area of social and economic development? Probably so, but only if its assumptions about economic growth are modified. Economic growth is not automatic; a favorable social as well as physical environment is prerequisite. In the past, TVA emphasized the physical aspects of the environment. As already pointed out, this did not automatically lead to desired changes in social and economic development.

The fundamental need of the region is to increase its income through more jobs, not only in natural-resources production, but in processing, manufacturing, and service industries. An appropriate climate for economic development is required. This in turn requires regional, state, and local action to create this favorable climate. TVA's major job is to help this happen.

Economic development depends not only on the productive potential of natural resources but also on their orderly development. Growth is necessary, but not at the cost of destroying the region's natural environment, with its potential for good living as well as the base for a recreational industry. Such potential, still present in the TVA region (adequate water, open spaces, etc.), has been destroyed or has deteriorated in many of the more industrialized parts of the country.

A good place to live is a prime factor in industry location. This implies removing and then preventing the further physical pollution of the natural resources, as well as removing and then preventing further social pollution, such as urban and rural slums and other evidences of social irresponsibility. Increasing population and urbanization will cause the deterioration of more and more areas unless this is prevented by foresight. Communities that permit pollution, that attract jobs with low tax rates or other inducements, that advertise docile labor forces, and communities that have no planning machinery, may be successful smoke chasers. They may attract jobs, but they may do so at the risk of postponing or even destroying their potential economic well-being. In the long run, conditions so perpetuated may leave the area below the average, economically. As other communities in the nation pay for correcting mistakes due to previous lack of planning and foresight, any community continuing to make the same mistakes will hardly be attractive as an ideal place to live. Most businessmen know that the remedial costs will only increase and will be paid by the community sooner or later.

The rich regions can afford to correct their mistakes or even to make new ones. The poor regions, if they wish to catch up, should benefit from the past and prevent rather than repeat others' mistakes. Those communities which recognize and prevent social costs are ultimately high-priority choices for the location of desirable private enterprise investment. Those communities which ignore social costs will get their larger share of the rejects of other regions, the less desirable entrepreneurs who charge a high price for their favors. Why ask for the less desirable business when one can create conditions suitable for the best?

If we assume that the region should increase its share of the national economy by taking advantage of the region's natural endowment, then TVA should have the responsibility to see that resources are developed without losses to the area, without social costs. State and local agencies should plan public development and set guidelines for private development that minimize environment pollution. TVA should help create an environment or social climate such that the best of private enterprise is willing to invest in the region.

A social climate that is inviting to industry and commerce implies stable local government capable of directing growth and change. It requires the amenities one expects of good government. Good government implies foresight. Good government, by means of adequate planning, anticipates and prevents problems from arising. Good government directs and controls land-use changes by whatever tools are necessary, so that the community is a good place to work, to live, to visit, or just to pass through.

What action is open to TVA if it wishes to have a positive role in developing a climate for growth that takes advantage of the region's endowments for better living?

Two areas need emphasis: (1) studies of the region's position in the larger economy, so that state planning and administration are coordinated and beneficial to the region; and (2) grass-roots guidelines for educating people to the problems of economic growth, industrialization, and urbanization. Support is necessary from both local and state government so that state and local planning and implementation will create the kind of social and physical environment that is good for business and people.

Many people in the region are close to the land and wish to remain so. To stay on the land and have income as well, they must have jobs. This depends on a climate for investment that will bring in jobs in competition with other areas bent on economic growth.

All TVA policies and programs should be oriented to creating a desirable climate for growth. Much greater effort is required to get local government to accept its responsibility for creating this climate. Much greater emphasis on the role of urbanization in the region is required, as well as increased education on the requirements of continuous planning and the need for coordination of responsible state and local agencies.

Bringing the TVA region up to the better practices of communities, states, and regions that have accepted public responsibility is a big order. The Knoxville area is an indicator of the magnitude of the problem. Until very recently, thirty years after TVA was created, visitors to Knoxville could still be surprised by the apparent lack of community acceptance of the need for stable government and ordered growth. It is as if TVA and its staff of experts had not existed. Yet, the Knoxville region is a major sector of the TVA economy.

If TVA takes responsibility for regional coordination of social and economic development planning activities, its own policies must be consistent. The following specific policy areas are discussed because current activities or statements do not appear to be consistent with the coordinating role that is required.

Agricultural Policy

TVA's statements and programs in agriculture imply that increasing productivity per acre and reorganization of farm systems are sufficient solutions to the problems of rural low income. Farmers can stay on the land and produce as much as possible to improve their income. All that is needed is a change of practices, use of fertilizers, and other capital improvements to increase productivity and income.

We have no quarrel with these statements when they refer to farm units that can provide adequate income if they adopt known practices. Water development and flood protection activities may make previously non-economic units capable of providing satisfactory income. No change in the acreage of the unit is required; no change in number of farmers is implied.

There is a problem, however, where a major portion of an agricultural area consists of units too small for full-time employment and adequate income. A proportion of these farms can become economic units by increasing their acreage at the expense of others, or they can be part-time farms with the additional income derived from non-farm jobs. Rural residence and part-time farming requires jobs within driving distance. If these jobs are not available, improving unit production to increase income, even though the income is still inadequate, appears justified as a short-term policy. Any additional income, due to increased production, is an improvement. But it is not a solution to the problem, and statements that imply otherwise are a disservice.

If jobs within driving distance are not available, the changes required to make farms into economic units cannot occur unless some farmers leave the area. And part-time farming is likely to be part-time unemployment.

It should be clear that one does not have to leave the land in order to get out of farming. Rural residence, with all or most income coming from non-farm work, does not require leaving the land or even changing ownership. The productive acreage can be leased to make some other units economic, or the acreage can be set aside in productive or protective cover for supplementary income.

The land problem, then, has several aspects: low income; the goal of continuous productive use of the land, if in farming; and the best use of the land in the larger regional context. There are three possible solutions to the problem of farm income:

1. Some farm units need only adopt existing practices to raise income. No change in the acreage of these units is required.

2. Some farm units need an increase in acreage by sale or lease to become economic units. This assumes that people in some small units must leave agriculture to make the necessary increases for others available. Whether the owners leave the area or not depends on their non-farm income.

3. Some farm units can only be part-time farming, and non-farm jobs are needed to provide adequate income if part-time farming is to continue. No change is required in acreage.

Jobs, then, are required, not necessarily in the county or in the watershed, but within driving distance. Here again, the need for good government in county and municipality to stimulate a climate that will be conducive to job creation should be emphasized. If rural area population increases faster than job opportunities are created, the only solution is moving excess population out of the area or providing welfare income. Where it is evident that sufficient jobs cannot be created in the foreseeable future, programs are required that will permit making the necessary land-use changes and population adjustments. Postponing these changes perpetuates the low-income problem. TVA should be a guide for potential development of land resources in relation to potential job development. It might also guide the education or training that is necessary if many are required to leave the area.

Agriculture is a regional problem, not a single watershed or county problem. Whether a given local area can be primarily full-time, part-time, rural residence, or a mixture of these should be a planned objective, not a result of chance, and should be considered in terms of farm labor opportunity cost relative to foreseeable off-the-farm jobs.

Coordination of four objectives is required:

1. The short-run objective of seeing that individuals increase their income with whatever resources are available—taking advantage of whatever federal aid programs exist.

2. Seeing that farm units provide full-time employment and give adequate income from land potential plus capitalization.

3. Seeing that all lands not in full-time economic units are productive, whether as part-time units or as leased parcels to economic units. This creates production and jobs in the area even if the land owner does not do the work. Used in this way, the small holdings may be prevented from fragmentation for rural residence and remain available for future agricultural production or other space uses.

4. Finally, recognizing other uses of land resources than agriculture that might enhance the area.

TVA must act as a guide not just for individual farms but for changes in the region, considering the national trends of agricultural industrialization as well as the trends in urbanization and industrialization of different parts of the TVA region. Any agricultural policy that does not consider these problems and trends is an oversimplification of resource development and economic development and may merely perpetuate poor land use and low-income differentials as they now exist.

Small-Watershed Program

TVA's interest in the tributary watershed program is twofold. First, it is a continuation of engineering development to control and make use of the entire Tennessee River system. It is an extension of integrated development and control to the smaller tributaries, each bit adding to the effectiveness of the entire system. Second, it is an approach to integrated resource development through grass-roots action. Central to the integrated development of all resources in an area is the control and development of its waters. A grass-roots approach based on the watershed seems logical.

Citizen organizations representing tributaries of 1,000 square miles or more are the units with which TVA cooperates. Watersheds of this size may run through several counties or cross state lines. For taking action on social or economic problems, how realistic are organizations whose boundaries are established by the physical limitations of the watershed? If the problems in the area are on the river (flood, pollution, erosion, etc.), the watershed area is the focus of common problems and interest. If the watershed is small enough, a neighborhood familiarity may exist; but the 1,000-square-mile watershed is too large to be neighborly and too small to solve social and economic problems that are widespread. Solutions may require action outside the watershed.

Some criticism has been raised that the primary objective of the program is large-scale construction on the small tributaries. Additional dams would enhance the total control system of the river but would not necessarily correct the low-income problems of the people in the area.

There is no program for tributaries smaller than those of 1,000 square miles. What of the metropolitan regions? The growth of the metropolitan area, based on marketing, transportation, and service facilities, depends on the social and physical climate. Effort here may be more important than similar effort on the small tributary. The small tributary may not be able to create jobs that are based on other than natural resources produced in the watershed, but the metropolitan region is the focal point for an industrial, distribution, and service complex.

Granted these limitations, can the tributary program be justified from the grass-roots approach? Representation on the tributary association is usually by county and municipality as well as by individual interest. The area is small enough so that members from all parts of the tributary can attend meetings. The county and municipality are the political units that must ultimately make decisions in planning resource use. When tributaries cross county lines, the association acts as the coordinating machinery across local political boundaries. This can also be true for state lines.

If state action or state aid is required, it is asked for, and then it is channeled through the county and municipality. Therefore, from the local and state viewpoint, the county and municipality are the units through which political action must be taken. Just as important, most federal programs operate through the county government, and aid requests must come from the county or municipality.

The TVA role in the small-watershed program is to help these citizen organizations recognize their problems, to help coordinate their efforts with those of national programs, and to coordinate their activities with other local units when problems or solutions cross political lines or are larger than their boundaries.

The small-tributary approach to the achievement of citizen education and political action is realistic; both are needed to make each area a better environment for economic development. However, the small-tributary approach does not add up to a total regional program. To be effective, the tributary program must be part of a larger effort. It must be the grass-roots planning and implementation of larger programs that include the main stream and the urban centers. The coordination of rural to urban, urban to region, and region to the entire economy requires competent state agencies to coordinate transportation, land uses, and other required institutions on all levels. The small-watershed program alone cannot be effective on problems that are larger than the watershed.

Industry Site Policy

Where industry sites are not plentiful or are costly to develop, high priority in location and reservation is needed. TVA has been concerned with this on its waterfront controlled lands; but regionally, it should be as concerned about other sites as well.

TVA or the states or both should create machinery for buying or reserving, by whatever techniques are appropriate, suitable areas of land for industry. The acreage should be based on studies of future requirements and should consider the trends of national markets, population, and other variables important in industry location.

TVA has been concerned with protection and creation of industry sites through engineering work on its tributaries, and it should try to get this objective more fully accepted as a benefit in benefit-cost analysis. A comprehensive industrial site program for the region may make it easier to justify this function as a benefit in water control. TVA should be equally concerned with proper highway location for this same purpose.

In its small-watershed association reports, attention is given to making the best use of potential industry sites within the watershed. However, the small watersheds do not cover the entire land area, nor do they provide grass-roots programs in the metropolitan regions.

Highway planning that takes advantage of the interstate highway system as well as development of the areas adjacent to the interstate system should be a TVA responsibility with the planning arms of the several states.

Dispersion of industry is necessary if there are to be jobs within driving distances of areas that are suitable for part-time work in farming—jobs in some forms of recreation, as well as in less intensive uses of land for forestry or recreation. Jobs within driving distance are required if lands in part-time or residence use are to be as productive as possible.

Highway Location Policy

Well-planned highway location now may be of greater value to the region than any other factor of industrial location or economic development. Highway location is as important in developing the recreational potential of the region as in the development of manufacturing industry. Recreation that brings outside funds into the region is job-creating and makes available internal funds for investment. Planned recreation development may enhance the region as a more desirable place to live and to locate new industry. A recreational industry, to be attractive to both outsiders and the people of the region, requires aesthetic considerations, not commercialization alone, in both the recreational developments and in the total regional environment in which the recreational industry is located.

Navigation and Water Policy

Navigation tonnage will increase, but TVA's emphasis on the relative importance of navigation to industrial development should be examined.

The trend of railroad specialization in order to be competitive with the public highway system offers alternative modes of transportation. Low-cost transportation, by whatever methods, is most desirable from the national standpoint. Fighting the railroads as if they were monopolies, as if conditions today were the same as those existing in the early days of TVA, is quixotic.

Clean water for industry, or clean water for a desirable living environment, may be more important than navigation for industry location. Pollution control and planning of water uses for non-compatible recreational uses is as important or more important than navigation. A navigation channel with scheduled lock opening and small boat owner-user fees might justify inland navigation for recreational use as well as commercial traffic. But water for industry and recreation should have priority over navigation. The TVA region may already have river site comparative advantage for the few industries that rely on water transportation. This comparative advantage may increase in the near future as locations become scarcer in other parts of the country. But emphasis on heavy industry on the river seems desirable only if the water resource is not damaged for other uses, and only if it has been considered in the framework of total regional development.

Staff Requirements for a Multilevel Coordination Responsibility

Public education to understand the region's potential and the need for planning to get it, creation of the necessary planning agencies on all levels and their acceptance of planning implementation responsibilities, and finally, the coordination role required in the complex of federal, state, and regional interest require a diverse staff. TVA does not at present have a large enough staff to do the threefold job required. The job varies from regional analysis and coordination to local help and guidance.

First, TVA needs an adequate staff responsible for studying larger regional problems, trends, and potential developments of national origin. They must be capable of working with the federal agencies and state planning units.

Second, TVA needs a staff to work in the field at grass-roots levels. They must be, in essence, an extension service. Creating citizen organizations, attending meetings, expediting the organization's activities—all are time-consuming. The businessman, political official, or other citizen representative in the association does not have full time to devote to the organization. Grass-roots efforts are slow and time-consuming; but only as people participate do they become self-educated, and only as they look into their local problems and work out their own solutions does local political action take place when needed.

Third, TVA needs a staff to give assistance in the analysis of local problems of the watershed and their solutions, considering the larger problems of the subregion or the TVA area in general. The staff must be capable of helping local units to recognize and take advantage of the federal aid programs that are available. They must be capable of seeing beyond the tributary so that the solutions to local problems move the region in the direction desired. Local action should give results that when added together are not disruptive, competitive, or ineffective for lack of broader program coordination.

Obviously, the staff required to help create a social as well as physical climate conducive to economic growth is many times larger than that which TVA has now. Having for years been on the defensive against congressional pressures and local and other criticisms, TVA is essentially a river- and power-management organization. Through the years, funds have been cut, staff has left, progress in planning has slowed or ceased. It may now be difficult to pick up momentum that once existed. A start in the small tributary program and the Land Between the Lakes recreation program indicates there are still touches of the old TVA.

However, to secure adequate staff will require a program that is challenging, since TVA is no longer unique nor the only market for young planners and economists. Planning commissions, regional authorities, regional studies, international projects of all kinds, and the new federal aid programs are competing for the same people. These people must be persuaded that TVA is not just another bureaucracy, competing against other public programs and newly organized bureaucracies.

If Congress can be persuaded to expand the expediting and coordinating role of TVA to do the necessary planning, educational, and coordinating work on regional, state, and local levels and if sufficient staff can be found for the job, then TVA as a social experiment in regional and grass-roots democracy can be very much alive and need not be consigned to the historical past.

References

1. The use of this model for economic development of underdeveloped countries has been questioned elsewhere in this volume. TVA should make it clear that coordinated, multipurpose river development is a desired natural resource development procedure but is not itself economic development, and that "TVA's" in developed and underdeveloped economies are quite different institutions.
2. Norman Wengert, *Valley of Tomorrow: The TVA and Agriculture*, the University of Tennessee *Record, Extension Series*, XXVIII, No. 1 (Knoxville: Bureau of Public Administration, the University of Tennessee, 1952).
3. On this point see the comments of Bruce Netschert in the first essay in this volume.

The Future of TVA

AUBREY J. WAGNER received a B.S. in C.E. degree from the University of Wisconsin in 1933. He held various positions in TVA from that time until 1954, when he succeeded John Oliver as General Manager. Mr. Wagner held that post until elevated to a directorship in 1961. In 1962 he became Chairman of the Board of Directors of TVA.

The lifetime of TVA has almost spanned a generation. Many of those who in the early 1930's fought the battles leading to the creation of TVA—the conservationists, the "farm bloc," the political leaders—have passed from the national scene or are stepping aside one by one. Most of the men who shaped TVA's first operating policies, designed its first dams, and produced its first fertilizers have been supplanted by others. The young people of that earlier time—those who watched while a river was placed in harness, while gullies were healed with well-fertilized cover crops, while electricity marched on new, life-giving wires across the land—today these people are grown; to their offspring, the physical transformation of a river valley is a fact of history.

It seems an appropriate time to present an assessment of TVA, in some respects with relation to the past but more generally in terms of its impact on the future. This, in effect, means an assessment of the future of the Tennessee Valley, for TVA's task from the beginning has been to help build a brighter future for this region. To this end we might seek answers to questions such as these: What is the state of our natural resources in the Tennessee Valley after three decades and what should be done to make them more responsive to human needs? What kind of life can we fashion from these resources? As we face the future, do we see a horizon of greater employment, improving business, expanding opportunity, and enlightened freedom?

Francis Bacon, the great English philosopher of more than three centuries ago who did so much to open men's minds to the idea of observing natural phenomena and learning from these observations, once wrote, "Nature, to be commanded, must be obeyed." The natural resources of the Tennessee Valley could not be commanded in 1933 because they had been dissipated. The abundant rainfall, instead of nourishing the land, washed it away. A river of immense usefulness was allowed to run rampaging in flood.

From TVA's creation more than thirty years ago, its programs of resource development have recognized the interrelationship of resources. If there is a single, overriding consequence from the TVA experiment in comprehensive valley development it is that resources can be developed in harmony, that they can be used without disturbing that harmony, and that their use in this manner can be the means of speeding economic growth and improving the quality of man's living.

The basic change in this region, therefore, is that its future no longer is dominated and depressed by the adverse forces of nature. Its resources are contributing to its growth. Nature is being commanded because it is being obeyed.

Resources—A Look Ahead

Progress in resource development, however, has itself created new problems in resource use. Our population has grown, and most of the growth has taken place in the cities. Demands on our resources are much greater, and conflicts have arisen as we attempt to use them for many purposes. Much of our future will depend on how well we work together to resolve these conflicts.

Stream Pollution. One of the most obvious and potentially a very serious limitation on our future is stream pollution. In terms of sheer quantity of water, the Tennessee Valley will have a plentiful supply for all foreseeable needs for years to come. A dependable 52 inches of rainfall each year will see to that. But the usefulness of our water supply can be curtailed or even destroyed altogether when cities and industries fail to treat wastes adequately prior to discharging them into the streams. On the whole, water quality in the Tennessee Valley now is as good as can be found anywhere, but there are spots where pollution is a problem and correction is needed even now—as in Fort Loudoun Lake. And as cities increase in size and as industries increase their use of the river for waste disposal, great vigilance and careful control will be required.

This responsibility now lies primarily with the state and local governments. Scores of cities in the region have taken active measures to reduce pollution. New industries, in the main, are taking care of their waste problems in conformity with modern standards. Each of the seven Tennessee Valley states has established its own pollution control agency. Recognizing the interstate nature of the problem and the extent to which cooperation is needed to solve it, they have recently joined in setting up an interstate compact; but so far only three states have ratified it.

Although industrial and employment growth is the primary economic stake in keeping our rivers clean, the public will come into personal contact with the problem, most frequently as it uses the waters for recreation. There are few areas in this country where fresh water lakes of the size and beauty of those in the Tennessee Valley reach literally to the doorsteps of our major population centers. Yet people cannot safely swim or ski in these lakes if the water is unclean. Polluted waters also limit opportunities for fishing. The most noticeable result of pollution, therefore, will be its effect on the enjoyment of the water and on the tourist business it can attract. A recreational asset of unparalleled attractiveness is one of the great stakes involved in our efforts to keep our reservoirs clean.

Transportation. A generation ago the Tennessee Valley was a land-bound region without access to economical water transportation. The Tennessee River reached deep into the heart of the Southeast. But the plagues of low water in summer and floods in winter made it useless as an artery of interregional commerce. Today the new Tennessee channel feeds traffic into and out of the whole Mississippi River basin. Industries locating in this area have many alternatives in meeting their transportation needs. Water carriers ply the rivers. Railroads criss-cross the region. Highway transport and service centers, already here in large numbers, will grow as expressways speed truck and bus commerce.

We have much to gain from encouraging the greatest possible coordination of these various modes of transport, because each has a kind of traffic for which it is best suited. Waterways can handle the large bulk cargo needs of heavy industry at extremely low basic costs. But obviously they can carry to and from only the riverside cities. Trucks and railroads can, however, work out joint arrangements, both as to rates and physical arrangements, which will extend to inland cities some of these benefits of the waterway.

This is the approach which I believe was envisioned thirty years ago by Joseph P. Eastman, one of America's most farsighted specialists on transportation. In 1934, in one of his early reports as Coordinator of Transportation, he wrote:

> Each form of transportation—rail, water, highway, pipe line, and air—can perform certain service more cheaply or more efficiently than any of the others. It should be protected in such service against destructive competition by the others, and at the same time provisions should be made for easy interchange and the establishment of through routes and joint rates where such coordination is desirable.[1]

Mr. Eastman made it clear that the test to be applied in achieving such a coordinated transportation system should be the public interest rather than any single private interest. His object was to provide service "at the lowest possible charges consistent with adequate maintenance and ability to provide the modern facilities and the character of service which the best interest of commerce and industry demands."[2]

After three decades, this policy is more important than when Mr. Eastman spoke, for transportation determines accessibility to markets, which is a major aspect of economic growth. Yet the policy still needs implementation, not only in this region but in the nation. I believe that in the coming years the Tennessee Valley can provide some leadership in the achievement of these goals.

Institutions for Resource Use

The state of our resources, however, is but the beginning. The real test of the future is our ability to use them properly and fully. And people use their resources well only when they have the means for working together through institutions geared to the task and operated under clear guidelines. The Tennessee Valley has such institutions—strong, reliable entities built up over many years.

Electric Power. In the field of electric power the local institutions are the distributors of TVA electricity. There are now 157 of them—102 municipalities, 53 rural electric cooperatives, and 2 small private distributors. We have worked together over the years—TVA as the wholesaler, the distributors as the retailers. Jointly, we have achieved a power system that operates at less than half the cost of the average electric utility in the nation. In consequence, rates are less than half the national average, and our home and farm customers use over twice as much electricity. We have shown that electric power can provide a vital, dynamic stream of economic activity that spurs the commerce and growth of the entire region. This is a force which must thrive and grow.

For TVA's part, we must search out the most economical and efficient methods of power production and distribution. The giant 900-megawatt generating unit now under construction at the Bull Run Steam Plant probably will seem small and antiquated in comparison with the plants we will be building when another generation has passed. I have no doubt that we will have a very significant proportion of nuclear reactors fueling our steam plants, and it is possible that even more exotic sources of electricity may then be in use.

Similar efforts toward economy and efficiency will be necessary on the part of the municipal and cooperative distributors. But the retail distributors have an additional responsibility which is one of the keys to our common future and to the Valley's future. This responsibility is the promotional education that keeps the public aware of modern effective uses of electricity and expands its use. And only as its use expands can it contribute to better living.

Here is the secret of continuing low rates. Only by achieving the highest possible consumer use can we keep reducing our unit costs of operation. Efficiency and economy are half the battle. The other half is the promotion of a mass market.

More than just the Tennessee Valley is involved in this task. Congress gave TVA a special job in producing and selling electricity. The TVA power system is a demonstration to the nation that power can be made available at low rates while maintaining the utmost financial integrity in the power system. Thus, the consumer interest of the entire country is involved in TVA's ability to maintain its record of low cost and low rates.

In the future, as in the past, success of the TVA power system must be measured in something more than kilowatt hours or dollars. More important is its devotion to our ideas and ideals of service to consumers, to the maintenance of more pleasant and more comfortable living, and to our national goals for economic growth. TVA power will live and remain vigorous only so long as this nation continues to recognize that freedom in business enterprise encompasses service enterprise in the consumer interest as well as profit enterprise in the private interest. TVA's greatest test will be its performance—its dedication to this consumer interest and the extent to which it lends strength to this concept of freedom in American enterprise. Effective competition by comparison in the electric power industry is a prime ingredient of our total national welfare.

Lake-shore Lands. The development of a river's resources for power production, or for navigation, or for flood control—or even for all of them together—is certainly not new in concept. Experience in the TVA programs has demonstrated, however, that in developing a river with dams and reservoirs we do create an entirely new resource which was not precisely foreseen. It is neither land nor water but a combination of the two. This is the shoreline of the TVA lakes. There are 10,000 miles of it, equal to the shoreline of the Great Lakes. Here is a resource of special value providing unique opportunities. But its use in the development of the region will also involve conflict, for it will be much in demand in the coming years.

Land which is oriented to the water has a particular usefulness for industry. Manufacturing processes are using water in their operations on an ever-increasing scale. Many industries find water transport highly desirable or even essential. In increasing numbers, new plants are finding it desirable to locate along the Tennessee, using the region's resources and supplying its expanding markets.

But the waterfront is also ideal for recreation, and the needs and demands for this sort of use are also growing. Resorts, parks, housing subdivisions, all are attracted to the lakes by the beauty of the surroundings and the excitement of water sports. Often the two—industry and recreation—run into conflict for the same space. And together they are sometimes in conflict with another force—the flood waters of the river itself.

Clearly, one of the important factors in the future of the region is the extent to which it is able to extract the highest value from its shoreline land. It can do so only by a process somewhat akin to the public rationing or allocation of a scarce commodity. It must be accomplished mainly by the people themselves, and fortunately the Tennessee Valley possesses the institutions of state and local government to provide the means for its accomplishment. These institutions are the state and local planning commissions and their staffs, and they are deserving of the highest priority of public support.

Along with wise planning, communities can put to use a wide array of legal instruments to guide and shape their growth and development. One of the important tools is the authority to establish zones for industries, businesses, housing, and recreation. Another is the power to establish standards for housing subdivisions. Still another is the layout and location of streets and sewers, water lines, and power facilities. All these are local, legal measures which can be applied on the initiative of local people and their representatives. Let us look for a moment at the problems and opportunities involved in the exercise of these local powers.

Safety from Floods. We have the science, the methods, and the experience to enable any city in the region to make itself virtually invulnerable to flood damage, if, together, we wish to make it so. It is a goal worth working for. But it involves more than protective works to keep the water away; it involves as well a willingness on the part of the community to keep its structures out of areas where the flood hazards are greatest.

TVA's system of flood regulation is the major bulwark against the great basinwide storms which sometimes wrack this area. But this system cannot prevent all flood damage. Many communities lie on the banks of small streams which are outside the zone of influences of the great reservoir system and which can erupt in a flash with watery devastation. Fortunately, through the hydraulic engineering sciences, we can now determine before a flood occurs how it will behave. We can tell how the worst floods will affect a community—the blocks into which it will reach, the depth and the swiftness of the current, and many other aspects. With these facts, if protective works are not feasible, cities can guide their growth away from the hazardous areas, using the legal measures mentioned above. Where buildings already exist in the floodway, various techniques of urban renewal are available as at least a partial remedy. Age and attrition bring down many buildings. Thus it is possible, over a period of years, gradually to relocate a community in a manner that will avoid flood damage.

Scores of communities in the Valley have worked with TVA and their state planning commissions to accomplish many of these objectives. Many others should; and the sooner they do, the more desirable and attractive their cities will be. In the Tennessee Valley we are—and we should be—working toward complete flood control. This will be when the greatest rainstorms sweep over the Valley and their waters pass out of the smallest streams and through the mighty Tennessee itself without damage, leaving the people unaware of the flood that might have been. I believe this day can come—though only after a long period of time and with the patience, willing efforts, and fullest cooperation among TVA, state, and local governments.

Industry vs. Recreation. Assurance against floods is itself an attraction to industry, but cities and counties can go further and use their legal powers to reserve desirable waterfront land for future industrial development. Good industrial land has certain distinct characteristics. It should be reasonably level, for example, and have good foundation conditions for economical construction. It should be near railroads and highways, as well as close to the water, so that both raw materials and finished products can be shipped in and out by the most advantageous means. Should land having these characteristics be preempted by homes or cabins or stores, the cost to industry for purchase and redevelopment would become prohibitive. A community which allows this to happen is depriving its future citizens of the jobs and payrolls and trade which future waterfront industry could provide. Planning and legal machinery should be put to work as soon as possible in order to allocate and preserve each section of the shoreline for the use which will contribute most in the long run to the people's well-being.

An outstanding example of this kind of planning is the work done by the cities of Oak Ridge and Clinton, with the Anderson County and the Knoxville Metropolitan Planning Commissions, in planning the shoreline of Melton Hill Reservoir. Before the lake was impounded, sites for industry, river terminals, parks, residential subdivisions, boat docks, and other uses were identified. In some instances excavation and construction of underwater facilities were completed in the dry.

Recreation, a constantly growing business in the region, also can benefit from planning. Not only is it an attraction for the tourist trade, but it is also an attraction to industry. Our lakes provide an outlet for wholesome fun and relaxation for employees and their families. Industrialists give substantial weight to this factor in selecting locations for new plants. In the Valley region the climate is moderate and adapted to a wide range of recreational possibilities. We can even make our own climate cheaply, since low-cost electricity permits low-cost air conditioning of businesses, homes, and indoor recreation establishments.

Indicative of the future involved in recreation development is the fact that our Great Lakes of the South already are used by the public with three or four times the intensity of the national parks. TVA has reserved for park and public access purposes hundreds of lake-shore areas totaling thousands of acres. Again it is up to the states and local communities to take the initiative in developing them, in upgrading their facilities to make them not only usable but attractive for the thousands—indeed, the millions—who will come. The space is there now. Its development for more intensive use is a task for the future.

TVA's demonstration work in the Land Between the Lakes is intended specifically to search out the kinds of development and activities which can make these outdoor recreation areas best serve the needs of our people in the coming era when we will be more and more industrial and more and more urbanized. In western Tennessee and Kentucky there lies an isthmus forty miles long and eight to ten miles wide, situated between TVA's Kentucky Reservoir and the future Barkley Reservoir on the Cumberland River. It is wooded land, sparsely populated. Congress has provided TVA with funds to develop here a huge outdoor recreation demonstration, now just getting underway. We hope to be able to show that such an area can be used for virtually every type of outdoor recreation: camping and hiking, and hunting of all kinds; wildlife conservation, including educational programs. The lake shores will be developed for boating, fishing, swimming, skiing, racing, and other water activities. We hope it will attract lovers of the outdoors by the thousands and that it will help to set standards for the design and development of others like it throughout the United States.

Forestry. Forests always have been and always will be of major importance in the Tennessee Valley. Fully 60 per cent of the Valley area is forested, and much of that land is essentially unsuited for any other use. Of our 26 million acres 15 million must contribute to our economy through their forests or they will contribute very little indeed.

Much progress has been made in the past thirty years in reforestation, forest fire control, improved woodlands management, and wood utilization. As one measure, the Valley produced about $100 million worth of wood products annually in the early 1940's. By 1960, the figure was $500 million and in 1963 it was $575 million. But the full potential has so far been only half realized. The same acres can be the basis for an industry turning out $1.2 billion worth of wood products each year, providing 150,000 jobs where now there are 50,000.

Present directions of effort must, of course, be continued. In addition, new and increased attention must be given to the hardwoods. They provide the basis for expanding furniture and other industries which are heavy contributors to the economy. With pine propagation quite well understood and underway, TVA is giving more intensive attention to selection, development, and propagation of superior varieties of black cherry, walnut, poplar, white oak, northern red oak, and chestnut oak. This is a program for the long-term future. In view of the ever-increasing demands for wood, the returns should be high.

The role of chemical fertilizers in forest management, a subject which TVA is peculiarly qualified to explore, is also receiving our attention. It, too, offers much promise for the future.

Agriculture. Valley welfare and national welfare in the future require a sound and prosperous agriculture. Over the years agriculture has provided the base for generating capital for much industrial development. Today, in regions which are predominantly rural, much of the capital needed for education, community services, and local industries originates in agriculture. In addition, we as a nation must continually confront the need to produce, on less land, more food and fiber for more people.

The national interests also are reflected in the private interests of our farmers. We notice year after year the steady growth of farm income. Today it is at an all-time high. But net farm income has continued to decline for the decade prior to 1959, while production expenses rose by 45 per cent.

For the individual farmer, this is the heart of the cost-price squeeze, demonstrating the need for more economical methods of agricultural production. Many farmers have fought it by applying the technology necessary to produce more on fewer acres. These are the farmers who will continue to farm. But another and less efficient group has only fallen further behind. These farmers—constituting 60 per cent of the total number and producing only 13 per cent of the total output—have very low incomes, own or control little land, and often possess too little skill or managerial ability to farm effectively.

What to do to help this low-income group is a problem of national concern. Many of them will drop out of the farming picture to take jobs in industry, their land going to enlarge neighboring farms. For those who continue to farm, however, fertilizer is one of the tools of hope as it is for their larger and more prosperous colleagues. And in TVA's chemical research center at Muscle Shoals, and in the experimental and educational extension facilities of the agricultural colleges, we have the organizational instruments to put our modern tools to work.

The future of agriculture in the Tennessee Valley offers a horizon in some ways cloudy but also with rays of light showing through. Less than 20 per cent of the workers in the Valley are employed on farms, compared with the national average of less than 10 per cent. Farms are smaller, averaging about 100 acres against 300 or so for the nation. And farm size is increasing more slowly—up only 31 per cent in thirty years, compared with the national gain of 93 per cent. Only 12 per cent of the farms sell $5,000 or more worth of produce per year, whereas 19 per cent in the Southeast and 48 per cent in the rest of the nation fall in this category.

On the other hand, significant strides have been made. Agriculture is more diversified and healthier. The value of farm products increased from $111 million to $547 million from 1940 to 1959. In percentage terms, the Valley held but did not enhance its competitive position with other areas. This, however, is a real accomplishment, since much of the area is mountainous and the small farms characteristic of this region tend to delay longest in the adoption of new technology. Output per acre in the Valley is comparable to the rest of the nation. But we have so many more people on the land that the output per person is low.

This is the crux of the agricultural employment problem in the Tennessee Valley. Even though the number of farms decreased by approximately 78,000 in the last ten years, there should still be about 70,000 fewer farms just to keep pace with national trends. Such large-scale population adjustment is difficult to achieve and painful to those whom it engulfs. The answer lies to a large extent in that combination of industrial and commercial growth which brings about steadily higher incomes. TVA is working in this direction. The people of the region are working in this direction. To create enough industrial and service jobs at a rate sufficient to absorb the overflow from agriculture is a task for all. It is the most difficult challenge this Valley faces.

For those who remain on the farm, programs of education and demonstration must continue. Recent innovations, in which entire geographic sections participated, give promise of increasing farm incomes more rapidly. In six counties of the Elk River watershed in Middle Tennessee we have seen a massive demonstration of soil testing and fertilizer use which, together with improved management, boosted farm income by several million dollars the first year. This effort was supported enthusiastically by both city and farm organizations. We believe that farm income in that area can be doubled to about $56 million annually and expect to achieve it in five years.

In western North Carolina a ten-year experiment in rehabilitation of mountain farming quadrupled farm incomes. I am confident, therefore, that with greater understanding of their own problems, individual farmers and their families will make decisions which will result in a better future for themselves and a healthier agricultural economy.

The difficult situation of the farm youth who must choose whether to remain or migrate can be eased in major degree if in our search for industry we obtain plants requiring high skills and responsibilities. Vocational training programs, if they are both effective and widespread, can make an important contribution here, assisting not only in taking up the slack of unemployment and underemployment but upgrading skills and incomes at the same time. High skills demand high wages and salaries. High incomes are the generating force for greater trade and commerce, and it is in the field of trade and commerce that the economy of the region is most deficient. The greatest source of additional employment in the future is in such fields as retail and wholesale trade, service industries ranging from laundries to television repair, insurance, warehousing, and hundreds of satellite functions that make up the essence of a prosperous economy. As we move to fill these gaps, we will provide for our young people what I believe to be one of the greatest gifts of a free, democratic society. This is the availability to young men and young women of a variety of choices as to what they may do with their lives. A society is not truly free if a young man must farm because his father farmed or must mine because his father mined. Freedom is achieved only when a combination of achievable education, adequate income levels, and variety of employment opportunities permit our youngsters to select and move into the field of opportunity which best suits their talents and ambitions as they appraise them. This is the real task for the future.

Tasks for Tomorrow

Now, if I may go back to my opening questions, I believe we can supply their answers.

Yes, we have abundant resources with which to fashion an economy of opportunity.

Yes, we have the institutions with which to mobilize our resources and put them to work effectively.

We need to devote more thought and energy, however, to the use of those institutions: (1) to improve our resources, intensifying our conservation efforts in the fields and forests, and with respect to water and its multiple uses; (2) to improve the agencies and organizations by which we work together and learn to use them more effectively; (3) to mobilize our talents and skills by careful inventory of the talents we now possess and by their nurture through education and training; and (4) to keep consumer interests foremost in our minds—in electric power, in transportation, in fertilizer for maintaining soil fertility. In so doing, we keep our economy always effectively competitive.

President Kennedy spoke to us at Muscle Shoals in May of 1963 on TVA's thirtieth birthday. He said, "The work of TVA will never be over. There will always be new frontiers for it to conquer. For in the minds of men the world over, the initials TVA stand for progress—and the people of this area are not afraid of progress."

Yes, there will always be new frontiers to conquer—frontiers as challenging and exciting as those we have passed. The touchstone for their conquest will be, I think, a continued seeking after excellence—excellence in our own performance; excellence in new fertilizers and in the quality of our forests; excellence in the quality of our waters and the ways we use them; excellence in our institutions and in their workings; excellence in every program, every research, every activity devoted to the well-being of those who now make the Tennessee Valley their home, and to those whom Senator Norris named "the generations yet unborn."

References

1. U. S. Congress, Senate, *Regulation of Transportation Agencies*, prepared by Joseph P. Eastman, 73rd Cong., 1st Sess., Senate Doc. 152, p. 12.
2. *Ibid.*

Index

Advertised procurement, 96–97, 100n
Agriculture
  extension programs, 31–32, 127–28
  food supply, 49
  policy toward, 134–37, 156–59
  trends in TVA region, 113, 126–29
Allis-Chalmers Manufacturing Company, 87, 89
Ansari, H. E. A. R., 38
Anticollusive bidding clause, 98–99
Appalachia, 52, 108

Bacon, Francis, 146
Baumol, William J., 96, 104n
Benefit-cost analysis, 66, 107, 110, 118, 139
Britten, Milton, 85, 102n

Cauca Valley Corporation, 29–33
  agricultural extension, 31–32
  flood control, 31
  organization, 30–31, 32–33
C. H. Wheeler Manufacturing Company, 90
Clapp, Gordon, 26, 28, 34, 40n
Commodity discrimination, 90, 95
Concerted action, 82
Coolidge, Calvin, 68, 110
Cordiner, Ralph J., 104n
Cost-benefit analysis, 66, 107, 110, 118, 139
Creeping socialism, 72, 76

Daniel, G. H., 10, 23n
Decision-making in politics, 59–63, 78, 118
Development and Resources Corporation, 34–36, 38–39
Dixon, Paul Rand, 85
Dixon-Yates controversy, ix

Eastman, Joseph P., 149, 160n
Ebtehaj, Abol Hassan, 34
Economic development
  concepts, xiv–xv, 68
  definition, 2
  heavy industry, 13
  sources of capital, 27–28, 32–35
Eisenhower, Dwight D., 72
Energy, electric
  alternate sources, 15–20
  demand estimates, 46–47

Fahey, Paul, 84–85, 93, 100n, 104n
Federal Power Commission, 67, 77
Fetter, Frank B., 104n
Flood control, 66, 152–53
  and CVC, 31
Forestry, 49, 155–56

Ganey, J. Cullen, 87, 88, 90
Garces Cordoba, Bernardo, 32
General Electric Company, 86, 89–91, 94, 95
Ginsburg, Norton, ix, xvn
Granger, Julian, 84–85, 95, 101n
Great Depression, 42, 53

Hart, A. B., 64–65, 79n
Hatch Act, 58
Hoover, Herbert, 68
Hubbard, M. E., 21, 23n

Ickes, Harold, 82
Identical bid awards, 97–98
Identical bids, 82–83, 84, 85, 86, 88
Industrial concentration, 94
Integrated river-basin projects, 19, 30–31, 108–10, 115–16
Irrigation, 36, 37
I-T-E Circuit Breaker Company, 87

Johnson, Lyndon B., 108

Katzenbach, Nicholas deB., 92
Kefauver, Estes, 85
Kennedy, John F., 52, 69, 91, 159
Kennedy, Robert F., 92
Khuzistan Water and Power Authority, 29, 33–40
  organization, 34–37
  training programs, 38–39

Lake-shore lands, 151–53
Lapp Insulator Company, 86, 87
Lasswell, Harold, 59, 61, 78n
Lilienthal, David C., 30, 34, 40n, 79n
Loevinger, Lee, 100n

Maass, Arthur, 65
Maher, William L., 85
Mergers, 95
Migration, 51, 52
Morgan, Arthur E., 82–83
Multipurpose projects, 19, 30–31, 108–10, 115–16
  and Dez River, 35
Mund, Vernon A., 87, 103n, 104n
Muscle Shoals controversy, ix, 63–67

National Association of State Purchasing Officials, 92
Negotiated procurement, 82, 104n
New Deal, 42, 69
Norris, George, 66, 160

Planning responsibility, 122, 141, 152, 154
Politics, definition, 58–59
Poverty in TVA region, 51–52, 108
Power
  electric
    and economic development, 4–9
    capital requirements, 9–11, 20–22
    demand for, 7
    in Iran, 37
    role of low cost, 5–7, 12–13, 107–8, 150–51
    steam generation, 7
  hydro, 18–22, 150
  nuclear, 17–18, 46–47, 150
Price competition, 94, 96
Price discrimination, 82, 94
Pricing
  f.o.b. plant, 82, 96
  multiple basing point, 82–83
  single zone, 95–96
Public Law 480, 33

Recreation, 44–45, 152, 153–55
Regional economic development, 52–54, 123, 125, 127, 129
  and TVA, 74–75, 128
Resources for the Future, 8–9, 44, 45, 55
Robinson, E. A. F., 10, 23n
Roosevelt, Franklin D., 11, 82
Roosevelt, Theodore, 67
Rural electrification, 14–15, 74, 150

Selznick, Philip, 71, 79n
Simon, Herbert, 60, 78n
Small watershed associations, 130, 131, 137–39
Social cost, 132
Socialism, creeping, 72, 76

Tennessee Valley Authority
  and private power, 67, 76–77
  and socialism, 72, 75–77, 126
  application of experience to underdeveloped countries, xiv–xv, 10–11, 26–40, 109–10, 116, 118
  attraction of industry, 7, 114–15, 129, 132
  criticism of, xiv, 6, 28, 124, 130, 134, 137

Tennessee Valley Authority (cont.)
  Dixon-Yates controversy, ix
  evaluation of, xiv–xv, 106–20
  industrialization trends in TVA area, 113–16
  management unity in, 27
  Muscle Shoals controversy, ix, 63–67
  personnel in Iran, 37
  policies
    agriculture, 75, 134–37, 156–59
    flood control, 66, 152–53
    forestry, 155
    industry sites, 139–41, 153–54
    lake-shore lands, 151–52
    navigation, 129, 140–41
    small watershed associations, 130, 131, 137–39
    unified administration, 75
    water, 140, 147–48
  political forces in founding of, 63–68
  political history since 1933, 69–73
  regional economic development, 74–75, 128
  rural electrification, 15
Transportation, 139, 140, 148–49
Truman, Harry S., 72

United Nations
  Food and Agriculture Organization, 32
  Special Fund, 32
Urban problems, 43–44

Vogel, Herbert D., 103n

Water
  flood control, 66, 152–53
  irrigation, 36, 37, 50
  pollution, 49–50, 132, 133, 140, 147–48
  recreation, 44–45, 50, 152, 153–55
  transportation, 148
Wengert, Norman, 79n, 126, 143n
Westinghouse Electric Corporation, 89, 94
White, Gilbert, 74, 79n
World Bank, 33, 39

The Economic Impact of TVA was designed by Helen Orton. The text type face is Linotype Times Roman, which Stanley Morison originated for *The Times* of London in 1932. Display lines were set in Alternate Gothic.

The book was composed by Heritage Printers, Charlotte, North Carolina, who also printed it on paper made by S. D. Warren Company. Carolina Ruling and Binding Company, Charlotte, bound the book in a cloth manufactured by Columbia Mills.

THE UNIVERSITY OF TENNESSEE PRESS